Emily Elizabeth Dickinson

Biographies by James Playsted Wood

Emily Elizabeth Dickinson

A Portrait

by

James Playsted Wood

Thomas Nelson Inc.

Nashville / Camden / New York

Library of Congress Cataloging in Publication Data

Wood, James Playsted, date
    Emily Elizabeth Dickinson.

    SUMMARY: A biography of the enigmatic Amherst poet who
during a life of seclusion produced some of America's most famous
poetry.
    Bibliography: p.
    1. Dickinson, Emily, 1830–1886—Juvenile literature.
[1. Dickinson, Emily, 1830–1886. 2. Poets, American]
I. Title.
PS1541.Z5W65   811'.4 [B] [92]   72–5903
ISBN 0–8407–6232–1

Acknowledgments

Quotations from Emily Dickinson in this book follow the texts of her poems as originally published in *Poems by Emily Dickinson, Edited by Two of Her Friends,* Mabel Loomis Todd and T. W. Higginson, 1890; *Poems by Emily Dickinson, Second Series,* edited by T. W. Higginson and Mabel Loomis Todd, 1891: *Poems by Emily Dickinson, Third Series,* edited by Mabel Loomis Todd, 1896; and *Letters of Emily Dickinson,* edited by Mabel Loomis Todd.

The writer's grateful thanks go to the trustees of Amherst College for permission to quote Dickinson material to which Amherst College owns the rights and, for assistance of various kinds, to E. Porter Dickinson, recently retired as research librarian of the Robert Frost Library of Amherst College; to Alexander H. Morton of the Frost Library; and to Margaret Rose, Associate Director of the City Library of Springfield, Massachusetts.

J. P.W.

for E.C.W.

Emily Elizabeth Dickinson

Preface

In this instance I will not forbear a personal note.

Once upon a time on a sunny day in late spring I was helping to proctor an examination in old yellow brick College Hall of Amherst College. The other proctor was George Frisbie Whicher. He carried a thick black binder, and occasionally, as we moved about among the silent students bent intently over their blue books, he opened it and carefully read some of its typed pages.

Suddenly he came up to me, handed me the binder, and said pleasantly, "Would you care to look at it?"

I had suspected what the binder contained and knew Whicher's for a courteous gesture, but I was embarrassed. I had been hired the year before to teach his course in American literature while, on sabbatical, he worked on his book about Emily Dickinson. The classroom and his office were close to each other on the ground floor of old Appleton Cabinet. When the doors of both were open, he could hear what I told his students. It had been an uncomfortable experience.

Gray-haired and handsome, an established scholar and a fine critic with a chill wit, George Whicher was a senior professor in the English Department. I was an instructor, held over on sufferance for a second year. It was the tag end of the Depression. I needed the job.

I knew Emily Dickinson's poetry well. Without consciously memorizing, I knew many of her shorter poems by heart. I had read, I suppose, all of the books that had been written about her up to that time. Anything that George Whicher wrote would be sound, but he had not done this kind of thing before, and I did not know whether he could do it.

I opened the binder clumsily. It would be impossible for me to comment honestly or even sensibly on the neatly typed manuscript. Praise would be ironically received. Any considered judgment I dared would seem like an impertinence.

I was uncomfortably aware of other things. George Whicher knew his subject, but it was dangerous to write anything about Emily Dickinson in Amherst. Everyone knew the red brick Dickinson mansion behind its high cypress hedge on East Main Street, and most of the townspeople knew something of the repeated Dickinson legends. A century earlier the very building we were in had been the First Church of Amherst, with Edward Dickinson as one of its leading parishioners. As a girl and young woman Emily Dickinson had sat here in her father's pew and sung from a Watts hymnal.

A familiar sight in contemporary Amherst was Martha Dickinson Bianchi, stick in hand, striding through the village or about the Amherst campus, with Alfred Leete Hampson her invariable companion. Biographer of her aunt and, after the original editing by Mabel Loomis Todd and Thomas Wentworth Higginson, editor of her poetry and letters, Madame Bianchi was the possessive high priestess of the Dickinson cult. I had met her once at a tea. Feuds, sprung of bitter jealousies, flourished in Amherst like mushrooms in the rank soil of windowless cellars. The Dickinson-Todd feud was as firmly established as the Pelham Hills.

As unhappy as the undergraduates suffering through their examinations, I read a few pages of *This Was a Poet*. I recognized Whicher's edged phrasing and his critical deftness, but did not really take in what I read. I felt he already regretted the impulse which had led to his showing me the typescript.

When I thought I had held the binder as long as seemed fitting, I gave it back to its owner and asked some weak question about the book's publication. Whicher chatted easily about that for a moment. Then, relieved—both of us, I think—we went back to our proctoring.

More biographies and more statistically impressive editions of the poetry of Emily Dickinson have been issued since that time. Emily Dickinson has become the property of textual editors, the subject of scores of graduate theses, the concern of majestic universities, which dispute possession of her manuscripts, and the helpless beneficiary of fund-granting foundations. Whicher's was the first full-length comment about her by an outsider equipped as a writer who was also a student of American letters. Though some of its material is now outdated, *This Was a Poet* remains one of the few intelligent books about Emily Elizabeth Dickinson.

The Poems of Emily Dickinson, edited from her manuscripts by Thomas H. Johnson, and Jay Leyda's *The Years and Hours of Emily Dickinson* are invaluable. Too many other studies have been solemnly dedicated to the minutiae of prosaic scrutiny—antithesis of the poet's insight, vital spirit, and irreverent wit.

Emily Dickinson thought and wrote much of immortality. Could she have seen her own, threatened first by melodramatic biographies, then by pedantic desiccation, I think she would have fled immortality itself to an even deeper seclusion than she guarded in Amherst, then quickened it with her mockery.

She is in no danger, of course, from one more attempt to see her and say something about her. Her poetry sees to that.

J. P. W.

1

Emily Elizabeth Dickinson was born in the Connecticut Valley village of Amherst in western Massachusetts, December 10, 1830.

It seems wisest to put that down right away. Not only is being born one of the basic and inescapable facts of any life, but it is also a certain fact in the life of Emily Dickinson. Much of the rest of what is known or believed about her is based on legend, rumor, gossip, and fantasy —what in 1596 Sir Philip Sidney called "the notable foundation of hearsay."

Not until after her death, May 15, 1886, and the posthumous publication of her poems did Emily Dickinson achieve the fame she had wished for so desperately and fled so effectively. Drama and melodrama had to be discovered, guessed at, or manufactured then to account for her unusual life and her unique work.

Conjecture and supposition have made her a woman of mystery. So she may well have seen herself at times, for she was intense and imaginative, but she was also capricious. Sometimes she seems to tell all in her poems and letters. As often she tells nothing, nothing you can pin down with logic. She could seem infinitely wise but, just as easily, childlike. She could thrust with knifelike irony, stun with bluntness, then dance off, as elusive as a glance of light. Emily Elizabeth Dickinson was often an enigma to those who knew her best. She is an enigma still. That is the fascination.

She was named for her mother, Emily Norcross Dickinson, who came from the even smaller village of Monson, some twenty-five miles southeast of Amherst. Bestowal of her given name about concluded the influence of mother on daughter—at least the daughter thought so, and more than once she said as much.

It was different with her father. The influence of Edward Dickinson on his daughter, as on all three of his children, was strong. It was lifelong, and it is as marked in Emily Dickinson's verse and letters as it was in her life.

A contemporary account once described Edward Dickinson as a "River God," a term used a century earlier to describe men of wealth and power who ruled the Connecticut Valley by political strength and force of character. Colonel John Stoddard, uncle of Jonathan Edwards, had been a River God in Northampton; General Israel Williams in nearby Hatfield, another. Edward Dickinson was a man of their hard stamp. He was a lawyer, a college official, a businessman, a politician, a commanding public figure, a Puritan churchman. Proud that he was of the sixth generation of his family in Amherst, grim-visaged Edward Dickinson all by himself was an almost irresistible force. From childhood, Emily Dickinson stood in awe of her father. It was the correct posture. He *was* awesome.

What became Amherst was originally the Third Precinct of the much older town of Hadley, adjoining it to the west, where there had been Dickinsons since 1659. Dickinsons were among the first thirty families that settled in Amherst in 1751. The first meetinghouse, which was, of course, the center of any eighteenth-century New England town, was built in 1753. An Ebenezer Dickinson was one of the committee of three who called the Reverend David Parsons to be its first minister. The same letter that summoned him voted forty shillings "to mr. [sic] Dickinson for his preaching with us one day and a half some time since."

The Third Precinct soon outstripped the parent Hadley in population. When, in 1776, it was separately incorporated and named for Britain's conqueror of Canada, it was already a center of rebellion. Three of the five men who constituted its Committee of Correspondence during the Revolution were Dickinsons: Moses, Reuben, and Nathaniel. Moses Dickinson also led the choir in the First Church, where the only musical instrument then was his pitch pipe.

By this time Amherst had additional attractions. In 1783 there were five taverns and eight other liquor dispensaries to serve a village of some seven hundred people, and a thriving distillery was turning out three thousand barrels of cider brandy a year. Small wonder that Amherst became a favorite meeting place for insurgent farmers during Shays' Rebellion in 1786.

The Dickinson family continued to rise in wealth and power. In direct line of descent were Nathaniel, Ebenezer, Nathan, Nathan, Jr., then Emily Elizabeth Dickinson's grandfather, Samuel Fowler Dickinson. With him began the dynasty that virtually ruled Amherst for three generations.

Emily Dickinson's grandfather, her father, and then her brother were successively "Squire Dickinson." A corruption of "esquire," squire was a title not officially awarded in New England villages and towns. It was won by force of character and used with respect for acknowledged town leaders. Thus Emily Dickinson was born to the provincial Puritan purple. She was, and knew that she was, of the undisputed aristocracy of a Massachusetts village, and not just any village but distinctive Amherst. Despite what she wrote in one of her best-known poems, Emily Dickinson was never a nobody. To be a Dickinson in Amherst was by definition to be a somebody.

Amherst was different from Hadley, Pelham, Sunderland, Leverett, Belchertown, and other nearby villages. It was different from larger Northampton, seven miles to the west and seat of Hampshire County. It was different and, its inhabitants were convinced, superior, largely because Emily Dickinson's grandfather and then her father made it so. It had a famed academy and, *mirabile dictu,* a college. Samuel Fowler Dickinson had seen to that.

Samuel Fowler Dickinson was born October 9, 1775, and twenty years later graduated with honors from Dartmouth College. For one year he taught in an academy in New Salem, then read law in the office of Justice Strong in Northampton, and began to practice in his native village. Quickly he became the leading lawyer in a litigious town. For fourteen years he was Amherst's town clerk. He served fourteen years in the Massachusetts General Court, first as a representative, then as a senator. For forty years he was a deacon of the dominant First Church. In 1813, as befitted its leading citizen, he built the first brick house in the village, the mansion with its spacious grounds on East Main Street not far from the village center where, later, Emily Elizabeth Dickinson was born.

Samuel Fowler Dickinson was intent on making Amherst a center of learning, and here he had a strong ally in another Amherst resident, who was also a member of the state legislature. Yale graduate, teacher, lawyer, and lexicographer, Noah Webster came to Amherst in 1812 to work undisturbed on his *American Dictionary of the English Language*. Already famous for his spelling books, Webster bought a house and six acres of land just off the Amherst common and quickly became influential in town and church affairs. He even wrote the constitution of Amherst's first Sabbath school.

The very year Webster came to Amherst, Samuel Fowler Dickinson and Hezekiah Wright Strong started a subscription for a school, to be known as Amherst Academy.

The town of Amherst has a spacious common after the manner of all older New England towns. Main Street runs east and west at the north end of the common, and the place where it is crossed at right angles by Pleasant Street is the center of the village. West of Pleasant, Main Street becomes Amity Street. There, on the south side of Amity Street, on land donated by the Reverend David Parsons, a three-story brick building was erected at a cost of $5,000. As Amherst Academy, it opened in 1814 with more students than any comparable school in western Massachusetts. Quickly it became known as a good school, which meant at the time that it was both educationally proficient and sound in Congregational doctrine.

In 1816 Noah Webster presented a bill in the General Court to incorporate Amherst Academy. Over the objections of other solons, who said there were already four academies in western Massachusetts, the bill was passed. Samuel Fowler Dickinson then petitioned the court for a grant of eastern lands for the academy. Before public high schools were developed, Massachusetts encouraged a system of private academies across the commonwealth and had made such grants to Groton, Phillips Andover, Deerfield, Hopkins, Milton, and other schools. Amherst

Academy was granted a half-township of land, six square miles, in the District of Maine and promptly sold it for $2,500.

Amherst Academy drew students from all over New England. One, in 1818, was Mary Lyon, a big, rawboned country girl of twenty-one or twenty-two from the village of Conway in the foothills of the Berkshires. Mary Lyon studied grammar, geography, and advanced rhetoric. In 1837 she founded her Female Seminary in South Hadley, just a few miles over the Notch in the Holyoke Range from Amherst. This school became Mount Holyoke, the first women's college in the United States. In time Emily Dickinson was to attend both the academy her grandfather helped found and the college created by one of its early pupils.

Samuel Fowler Dickinson was so delighted with the success of Amherst Academy that he gave more and more of his time and energy to it and less to his law practice, which began to slip. In 1818 he and the other trustees of the Academy strove to collect $10,000 for the education of "indigent young men with the ministry in view." They found that people would give more willingly for a college than for an academy, so when they had collected more than $51,000 they voted to found the Collegiate Charitable Institution of Amherst.

The First Church raised all of the Charitable Institution fund, its leaders subscribing more than $10,000 of it themselves, with Samuel Fowler Dickinson one of two men who gave bond for the rest. In this sense, both Amherst Academy and Amherst College were born of the First Church.

There was plenty of precedent for the development of a college out of an academy. In 1636 Harvard sprang from a school kept in Newtown (Cambridge) by Nathaniel Eaton. Dartmouth succeeded a school for the Indians founded by Eleazar Wheelock in 1754. Williams College had been the Williamstown Free School. The Academy for the Education of Youth, which Benjamin Franklin founded in Philadelphia, became first the College of Philadelphia, then the University of Pennsylvania.

Competition for the intellectual distinction and material advantages of a college was strong among the towns of New England in the early nineteenth century. Amherst enthused, and its people turned out en masse to build South College, first of the Charitable Institution's buildings, on the hill opposite the First Church. They carted in the lumber, bricks, and mortar, camped on the grounds, and built it from cellar to roof.

Noah Webster gave the dedicatory address when the cornerstone of South College was laid, August 20, 1820. Academy trustees, clergymen from neighboring towns, contributors, those who had worked on the building were all there. The academy marched its students from Amity Street to the top of college hill. Little more than a year later, September 21, 1821, the Charitable Institution opened with the Reverend Zephaniah Swift Moore, who had fled the presidency of Williams College, as president. There were three instructors and forty-seven students. Noah Webster said now, "We do hope that this infant institution will grow up to a size which will contribute to check the progress of errors which are propagated from Cambridge."

Piety was the primary intent of Samuel Fowler Dickinson, Noah Webster, and the other First Church founders of the Charitable Institution. Harvard, in Cambridge, preached heretical Unitarian doctrine, and they would have none of it. Harvard, likewise, wanted none of Amherst. When the Collegiate Charitable Institution petitioned the General Court for a charter as Amherst College, Harvard, Brown, and Williams united in bitter opposition to its being granted. Samuel Fowler Dickinson fought back just as bitterly, and Amherst College got its charter February 25, 1825. Neglecting his other and more profitable interests, he worked as hard for it and gave to it as liberally as he had worked and given to Amherst Academy.

The Dickinson preeminence, the red brick mansion on East Main Street, Amherst Academy, Mount Holyoke College, Amherst College—her entire Dickinson-created village universe—were all waiting for Emily Dickinson when she was born.

2

Edward Dickinson, Emily Dickinson's father, was born on New Year's Day, 1803. He was the oldest of the nine children of Squire Samuel Fowler Dickinson. Naturally the "young squire" was sent to Amherst Academy and, as naturally, to Yale. Yale was the center of orthodox Congregationalism, and its degree carried greater prestige than one from his father's rural and isolated Dartmouth.

Edward Dickinson went to Yale as a provincial young gentleman of family, son of a prosperous lawyer who was also a public figure, a deacon of the church, and a patron of education. At least once the serious young student, who had been brought up to consciousness of the Dickinson place in the world, traveled to New Haven in the family chaise. The Dickinsons always had good horses.

When Amherst College opened, he was enrolled there, as a gesture of his father's faith in the new institution, which was in large part his achievement. Edward Dickinson spent his junior year at Amherst, but shrewdly returned to Yale for his final college year. It was there he met Emily Norcross of Monson, who was attending a young ladies' finishing school.

Determined and controlled even as a young man, Edward Dickinson took his Yale degree, then returned to the town of Amherst to study law with his father and at the Northampton Law School. He was admitted to the Massachusetts bar in August 1826, began to practice law a month later, and in May 1828 married Emily Norcross. She was deeply religious and domestically inclined. Strong, erect, sternly dignified, Edward Dickinson lived a man's life in the hard world of law and duty. He wished his home to be orderly and well run, a fit place for God and Edward Dickinson. His daughter, who worshiped him, felt that often he did not distinguish between the two.

The first child, William Austin Dickinson, was born in the brick mansion in April 1829. Emily Dickinson was born there a year and a half later. Then there was a hitch in the affairs of the Dickinsons.

Samuel Fowler Dickinson had worked not wisely but too well for his academy and his college. He had devoted too much time to the legislature in Boston and to the First Church in Amherst. His private business faltered, then collapsed. The situation so deteriorated that in 1833 he was forced to sell his splendid home to General David Mack, Jr., a fellow deacon of majestic manner who manufactured straw hats and had earned his title in the Massachusetts militia. Forsaking all of his interests and his position in Amherst, the fifty-eight-year-old Samuel Fowler Dickinson disappeared into what for him was virtual exile. He became fiscal agent for Lane Seminary in Ohio and later at Western Reserve College.

If Edward Dickinson felt this severe blow to Dickinson prestige, it is unlikely that he showed it. He never showed much. All he did was redouble his hard effort at the law, undertake his inherited responsibilities to Amherst College, and succeed and then outdistance his father in Massachusetts politics.

His three children—Lavinia Norcross Dickinson was born in 1833—were too young to be fully aware of the change in the family fortunes, and for some years the

Dickinsons continued to live in a rented part of the mansion. Emily Dickinson was ten years old before the family moved to a large white clapboard house on North Pleasant Street. Anyway, the house mattered less than the man in it. The children were intensely aware of their grim-visaged father.

Edward Dickinson had been not quite twenty-eight years old when his first daughter was born, but he never seemed young to her or to Austin and Lavinia. To them, as to the townspeople of Amherst, he personified strong convictions, integrity, and rigid austerity. Already he was a presence, and formidable. Amherst knew it when he marched to and from his office wearing his glossy beaver hat and carrying his gold-headed cane. There was a touch of fear in the respect accorded Edward Dickinson. Instinctively perhaps his children reognized what others knew but could not define. Edward Dickinson's forbidding reserve came of stern control which he could seldom relax, but it could not hide the passion and vibrant life in the man. He was independent, ambitious, responsible, but not without imagination. If the repressed power in him had ever been loosed, it would have crashed out in Jove-like thunderbolts.

The children also knew something else. He loved them and their mother deeply.

When Edward Dickinson was in Boston on business and later serving in the House of Representatives of the General Court, 1837–1839, and then in the Senate, 1842–1843, he wrote home frequently with worried affection and constant concern. He urged his wife to be careful and not to overdo. He entreated the children to obey their mother and help her in every way they could. He begged them all not to get sick. Every time he came home he brought small presents to his children, promising the best present to the one who had been best behaved.

" . . . Austin, be careful, & not let the woodpile fall on you—& don't let the cattle hurt you in the yard, when you go with Catharine, after water. Take good care of Emily, when you go to school & not let her get hurt." This note enclosed in a letter of January 17, 1838, to his wife was typical of many more. He subscribed to a religious paper for his children and also to a children's periodical, *Parley's Magazine,* for them.

Seven-year-old Emily Dickinson missed him badly when he was away and said she was tired of living without a father. He missed his children as much, and when he was at home he took them on picnics to nearby Mount Toby and other favorite spots.

Much of what Edward Dickinson was, Emily Dickinson became. The strength and surging life force were in her, too. She was independent, determined, and, in her own way, fiercely ambitious. She had her father's single-minded devotion to truth as she saw it. She repressed outward display of her emotions to increase their inner intensity. There was one difference. She would give rein to her imagination and free play to her piercing wit.

Irvin S. Cobb once said that George Horace Lorimer, famed editor of *The Saturday Evening Post,* was one of the great human nouns of his time. Edward Dickinson was a noun, an outstanding and upstanding fact of his daughter's existence. Emily Dickinson became a verb, a short, sharp, penetrating verb.

3

With the other village children, Emily, Lavinia, and Austin Dickinson learned their letters in the school on the Amherst common. They played with the offspring of teachers in Amherst Academy and of professors in the college. They grew up through the long, cold New England winters that deep-drifted the snow on the common, and through breathlessly still long summer days when the hum of insects was the only sound in the village.

There were sleigh rides in winter, the bells merry, their own and the horses' breath white in the arctic air. There were picnics in the fields and woods in summer. Winter or summer, they attended church and Sabbath school all day every Sunday. Emily Dickinson breathed in Puritan dogma as naturally as she breathed the flower-scented or ice-sharpened Amherst air. The tunes and rhythms of hymns became as familiar to her ear as the bird songs in which she delighted.

While Edward Dickinson was forging ahead in the law and town politics, hardily restoring the family fortune, and working as treasurer of Amherst College, his children were growing accustomed to the world like any other children of the time and place. An early portrait of the Dickinson children painted by an itinerant artist shows all three with the same boyish haircut, Emily's dark-red hair parted on the left side, her eyes large. If the scissors of Charles Temple, who cut a silhouette profile of Emily Dickinson in 1845, are to be trusted, she had a slightly bulging forehead, a snub nose, full lips, and a receding chin. She was not a conventionally pretty small girl. She would never be conventional about anything.

In 1841, when Emily was eleven years old, she and the younger Lavinia entered Amherst Academy. Here the vitality, the eagerness, and the distinctness of Emily Dickinson began to manifest themselves. Red-haired, brown-eyed, she was small, frail, and slight—and from the beginning a little fey. In those years the academy was an excellent school. Intellectually, morally, religiously, and socially it was a lively place. Its principals were young Amherst College graduates, and many of its teachers were Amherst seniors headed for the ministry. A preceptress looked after the girl students. Awesome Amherst professors lectured on botany, German, zoology, ecclesiastical history, or whatever their special subjects were.

Emily Dickinson was in love with all of her teachers, male or female, and enjoyed whatever they taught. Gay and vivacious, she was the unbridled enthusiast. She was in love with life as she was beginning to realize it, and here in books and people was the whole wonder of it, all the mystery, marvels, and miracles. A fascinated scholar, she studied Latin, French, and German. In one term or another she took Euclid (geometry), astronomy, algebra, and "mental philosophy."

She was so intent on taking in all of life all at once that she made herself ill. Her schooling was several times interrupted by recurring illness. After a particularly severe attack of influenza in 1846 her father sent her to spend several months recuperating with relatives in Boston. The next term she was back at Amherst Academy hard at work on botany, moral philosophy, geology, and Latin.

As might be expected, she excelled in English composition, required every second week. Oral book reports came on the alternate weeks, and she found the reading and reporting almost as exciting as writing.

The seven packed years that Emily spent in Amherst Academy were marked by her intensity and the enthusiasm she gave not only to her studies but also to parties, dances, her flower garden, and her full life at home. There was often company. Dickinson and Norcross relatives came and stayed for long visits. Emily and Lavinia and their mother had preparations to make before they came and work to do when they left. Emily disliked housework but loved cooking. It was a creative activity. There was something to show for her effort. She became known for her bread and a few years later took first prize for her loaf of rye and Indian bread at the annual Cattle Show.

She took piano lessons and exulted when her father bought a piano for their home. She entered with zest into the social and literary activities of a group of bright girls, most of them older than she, but she played her part as a Dickinson. That meant driving in the family carriage with its cream-colored upholstery, oval side windows, and folding top, and making formal calls with her mother in the elegant parlors of other families in Amherst's proper and dignified society. The carriage must have been drawn by a more sedate animal than the one Emily's father usually drove. As if he had inherited a touch of sporting blood from some worldly ancestor, Edward Dickinson had a taste for speed, and he vied with Deacon Luke Sweetser, merchant and relative by marriage, in having the fastest horse in town.

Politics was often the subject at home. Emily Dickinson heard it discussed hotly night after night by her father and the other lawyers, editors, professors, and ministers who came to confer with him. By the time she was fourteen she was, like her father, a convinced and defiant Whig (Republican).

That was one of the important facts she announced in a letter to her school friend, Abiah Root, February 23, 1845. The rest of the letter was filled with girlish sentiment, village gossip, characteristic humor, and even a touch of the sharp irony she was learning to perfect. "I keep your lock of hair as precious as gold and a great deal more so. I often look at it when I go to my little lot of treasures." She wishes Abiah would come and pay her a long visit.

> Miss ——, I presume you can guess who I mean, is going to finish her education next summer. The finishing touch is to be put on at Newton. She will then have learned all that we poor foot-travellers are toiling up the hill of knowledge to acquire. Wonderful thought! Her horse has carried her along so swiftly that she has nearly gained the summit, and we are plodding along on foot after her. . . . We'll finish an education sometime, won't we? Then you can be Plato, and I will be Socrates, provided you won't be wiser than I am.

Already Emily knew how to write effectively. A few months later she wrote Abiah that both Miss S. T. and Miss S. had married, that Dr. Hitchcock, president of Amherst College, had moved into his new house, that Mr. Tyler, who lived across the street, was moving into the old Hitchcock house, and that Mr. C. was moving into what had been the Tylers'. Vinnie (Lavinia) had gone to Boston with their father. Her plants looked fine. Abiah should start an herbarium, all the girls were doing it. She sent her a geranium leaf to press for her. She warned Abiah not to behave too well and to be herself in the Springfield school she now attended. "I expect you have a great many prim, starched young ladies there, who, I doubt not, are perfect models of propriety and good behavior. If they are, don't let your free spirit be chained by them."

Then in the same latter, May 7, 1846, when she was fifteen years old, Emily wrote this:

I am growing handsome very fast indeed! I expect I shall be the belle of Amherst when I reach my 17th year. I don't doubt that I shall have perfect crowds of admirers at that age. Then how I shall delight to make them await my bidding, and with what delight I shall witness their suspense while I make my final decision. But away with my nonsense. . . . All the girls send their love.

Like any other girl her age, Emily Dickinson was keenly aware of her appearance, and her compelling interest was boys. The academy and the college were full of boys and young men, some of them handsome, all of them promising, and most of them possibilities as husbands. "All the girls," including Emily Dickinson, who was precocious in most things, were well aware of all the boys.

The next year she was in Boston with her Norcross aunt and cousins. The great city was a revelation and a glory to behold. She went by train and delighted in the cars. The Chinese Museum, Bunker Hill, concerts, a horticultural exhibition—like any tourist, she did all the sights, and like many of them, climbed to the top of the State House. She was taken to see Mount Auburn in Cambridge and thought the famed "City of the Dead" was beautiful. "It seems as if nature had formed this spot with a distinct idea of its being a resting-place for her children, where, wearied and disappointed, they might stretch themselves beneath the spreading cypress, and close their eyes 'calmly as to a night's repose, or flowers at set of sun.' "

The thought is commonplace. The sentiment came from the First Church and the verse from Amherst Academy. Yet the schoolgirl showed a sharp awareness of death, which she retained. The Dickinson home on North Pleasant Street was opposite Amherst's West Cemetery. She saw the funeral processions come and go and observed people taking flowers to the graves on Sunday afternoons. She heard the burial services. In orthodox Puritan Amherst, Emily could not avoid knowing that this life is but a preparation for the next.

The long stay in the wonderland of Boston over, she was back in Amherst again. Her love of books was encouraged by her teachers and especially by the school's young principal. She needed no encouragement to play. Though younger than many of the others, she became the leader of a group of spirited young girls. Austin's friends as well as her girl companions were in and out of the big Dickinson house.

There were long country walks, valentine parties, candy pulls, parties at which, unknown to their disapproving parents, the young people danced. There were sugaring-off parties in Sunderland. Peculiar to the maple-sugar country of New England, where it is observed still, sugaring off is the pouring of warm maple syrup on snow saved for the occasion until May or June. Demure, bright, quick, Emily laughed and licked the spoons, dashed off comic valentines, raised her flowers—and was a zealous member of the Shakespeare Club, which insisted on reading unexpurgated editions of his plays.

The passage of the seasons and the ceaseless and indifferent progression of time awed Emily Dickinson always.

She moralized on it and quoted the very highest authority to Abiah Root. "For God has said, 'Work while the day lasts, for the night is coming in the which no man can work.' " You could not live in mid-nineteenth century Amherst without subscribing to this philosophy, but Emily Dickinson paid it more than lip service.

Fortunately for her and all the others, the Amherst seasons were broken by annual excitements. One to be anticipated and dreaded was the end-of-term exhibitions at Amherst Academy. These were oral examinations and demonstrations of the prowess of both students and teachers. Emily Dickinson looked forward to this event with tremulous expectation. Declamations, adjurations, the solemn reciting of maxims of wisdom, music, poetry, and Latin were all part of the exhibition.

Emily feared the exhibition, then determined not to fear, studied gaily, gave fearful attention to the selection of a dress and the arrangement of her hair; she lived in mingled excitement and panic. She had to do well, for her intense hope now was to go to the female seminary which Mary Lyon had opened in South Hadley.

Other annual events brought the same feverish anxiety about clothes and appearance, but no dread at all. One was the Cattle Show held on the common. Amherst was a farming town, as were Pelham, Plumtree, Sunderland, the Hadleys, Belchertown, and all the other towns and villages around. The Cattle Show brought in all the farmers with their wives and children, as well as college professors, local dignitaries, fortune-tellers, sideshows, and vendors of confections and souvenirs. For many years both Edward Dickinson and his wife were active as heads of Cattle Show committees and as judges of stallions, flowers, jellies, pies, and cakes.

Everyone came to see the prize cattle, the biggest pumpkins, the plowing matches, the workhorses, and the riding or driving horses brushed and currycombed until their coats shone. There were processions and blaring bands as the judges solemnly conferred. Emily loved the crowds and the noise. She thought the cows and horses beautiful and was as thrilled as any girl in the village at the fun of the fair.

Amherst College was a basic fact in the life of Emily Dickinson. It touched her daily. Its presidents sought the counsel of Edward Dickinson, who was not only treasurer but also a trustee and in charge of the building program of the college. He spoke for the college in the legislature. To a large extent the welfare of the college and the tenure of faculty members depended upon him. Presidential and faculty wives sought the distinction of being entertained by or receiving the wife and daughters of Squire Dickinson. Helen Maria, daughter of Professor Fiske, who taught Latin and Greek and later metaphysics, was one of Emily's childhood playmates, and the sons and daughters of other professors were her closest friends.

Similar to the junior prom of today was the senior levee. Weeks of anticipation came first for Emily Dickinson, then the breathless actuality as she was escorted to the great event by some greatly daring senior. It took courage as well as desire to invite the elder daughter of Squire Dickinson, then call for her under his watchful and forbidding eye.

Greatest event of the college year, of course, was commencement, and here Edward Dickinson and his family played a featured part.

Every year Edward Dickinson held his trustee's reception on the Wednesday night of commencement week.

The Dickinson home bulged with guests who came to stay with them at this time, and on Wednesday evening it was jammed. Governors and their uniformed aides, judges, editors, visiting dignitaries, and shy young men crowded into the Dickinson home. It was a dazzling display of dress and courtly manners, of brilliant conversation and well-bred laughter. The elite of Amherst mingled with the great of the larger world in what must have seemed to the young Emily matchless splendor.

The college came even closer when Austin Dickinson entered in September 1846. "Only think!" Emily Dickinson wrote Abiah Root. "I have a brother who has the honor to be a freshman."

Austin became a member of Alpha Delta Phi, the first national college fraternity to have a chapter at Amherst, and brought his brothers home to meet Emily and Lavinia. By this time Emily herself was dreaming of college. "You cannot imagine how much I am anticipating in entering there," she wrote her friend. "It has been in my thoughts by day, and my dreams at night, ever since I heard of South Hadley Seminary. I fear I am anticipating too much, and that some freak of misfortune may overtake all my airy schemes for future happiness. But it is in my nature to anticipate more than I realize."

By March 1847 she was reviewing arithmetic as well as taking higher mathematics and history in preparation for her entrance examinations. She deplored the loss to the academy of "our dear teacher, Miss Adams," but consoled herself that the preceptress had left to marry "a very respectable lawyer in Conway, Massachusetts." Soon she was equally impressed by the new preceptress, Rebecca E. Woodbridge, but it was the young principal who seems to have influenced her most.

In his early twenties, Leonard Humphrey was a graduate of Amherst College and a fraternity brother of Austin. Emily Dickinson was in love with him in the sense that she wrote, "I am always in love with my teachers." She called him her "master."

Humphrey later left the academy and the village to study for a year at Andover Theological Seminary; he then returned to Amherst College as a tutor. Seemingly well, he died unexpectedly November 30, 1850. His death was to be a severe blow to Emily Dickinson.

4

Emily Dickinson's foreboding that some freak of misfortune might demolish her dreams proved gloriously false. She graduated from Amherst Academy and in mid-September 1847 entered the South Hadley Female Seminary.

She knew all the excitement and trepidation of any not-quite-seventeen-year-old college freshman and, being Emily Dickinson, felt a dozen conflicting emotions at once as she became one of nearly three hundred young women held by stringent regulations to a strenuous regime. She landed in South Hadley tired from the carriage ride and suffering from a bad cold. These conditions did nothing to ease her nervousness as she began three days of entrance examinations.

Failure was unthinkable, a disgrace for her and her family. Success meant that she could enter the middle class at Mount Holyoke after a review of the junior work. The examinations were not easy, for Mary Lyon proudly set high standards, but Emily Dickinson passed them all without difficulty. She was exhausted then and violently homesick. Home was only seven or eight miles away, but, except for her extended stay with relatives in Boston, this was her first separation from it. Although she could go home for holiday visits, she would be away an entire year, which seemed to stretch endlessly into the future.

From the start she had little time to indulge her homesickness. Mount Holyoke girls got up at six o'clock every morning, breakfasted at seven, began study at eight, and met in Seminary Hall at nine for worship and prayer. Whether at Amherst or Mount Holyoke, piety was a central part of the curriculum. All intellectual endeavor was based on it and was meant to increase and enhance it.

At half past ten in the morning Emily Dickinson went to class for a review of ancient history. In another class at eleven she gave her interpretation of passages from Pope's "Essay on Man." Fifteen minutes of compulsory physical education came then, and that was followed by a brief interval for reading before midday dinner. As everywhere in New England, dinner came in the middle of the day, and, to Emily's surprise, it was good. She had heard the usual reports of horrible food that circulate in any school or college dining hall, but the food at Mount Holyoke was excellent and plentiful, the menu pleasantly varied.

Like the other students, Emily had assigned tasks, but hers, she admitted with some surprise, were hardly arduous. She had to clear the knives from the first row of tables after breakfast and dinner and to wash and dry them after the evening meal.

The devil found no work for idle hands at Mount Holyoke. Mary Lyon saw to that. The afternoons were as packed as the mornings. Singing lessons and piano practice kept Emily busy until half past three. After that came "Sections" in which each student gave an account of her conduct and activity during the day and confessed all lapses from grace such as being late or whispering during silent study hours. At half past four the students met again in Seminary Hall, this time to listen to sage counsel and religious exhortation from Miss Lyon herself. Supper came at six o'clock, and from its close until a quarter to nine there were silent study hours. The retiring bell rang then, but it was only a warning. Obligatory lights-out did not ring for another hour.

Emily Dickinson had feared being thrown with strange girls, some of them probably uncouth. Instead, she found herself among congenial companions. Her roommate was Emily Norcross, a Monson cousin and a senior. "She is an excellent room-mate and does all in her power to make me happy," Emily Dickinson reported. She missed her old friends, but, in her own words, she soon came to love many of the Mount Holyoke girls. Emily Dickinson was by nature a social creature to whom intense friendships meant much.

So did the outside world. She kept insisting that she loved Mount Holyoke, but she badly missed the dinner-table talk at home about Amherst, state, and national affairs. She felt she had not been made for life in a convent. Indeed, she told Austin, she felt as if she were living in a trance. Who was the candidate for President? She had been trying unsuccessfully to find out ever since she arrived at the seminary. Was the Mexican War over yet? Had the United States lost? Did he know of any nation about to besiege South Hadley? Both she and Austin knew that she was jesting, but they also knew that she was not jesting at all. Emily Dickinson at sixteen, thirty, or fifty was often most serious when she seemed most flippant.

The first homesickness went, but it was simply overlaid with new excitements and discoveries in a new environment and was easily provoked. Emily Dickinson's home ties were strong and deep. Lavinia, Austin, and she were close, and in a different way they were all close to their father. Austin understood. Emily Dickinson had been away only two weeks when he drove over the Holyoke Range to see her, bringing Lavinia with him. Emily was delighted when they came and even more delighted when they confessed they missed her.

About a month later she was looking out the window of her room toward the hotel when she spied her father and mother, come on a surprise visit, walking toward her. "I need not tell you," she wrote Abiah Root, "that I danced & clapped my hands, & flew to meet them." She hated to see them leave, but there was hope. "Only to think that in 2½ weeks I shall be at my *own dear home again.*" She counted the days and then the hours.

For once the reality when it came was as wonderful as the anticipation. Emily Dickinson's first college holiday was unalloyed joy. Austin came for her, and they drove back to Amherst in a downpour of cold, wind-driven rain. All the rest of the family, even the cat, were at the door of the North Pleasant Street house to greet her when the carriage stopped, her mother with tears in her eyes. Her father's grim features were relaxed. "Never," she wrote, "did Amherst look more lovely to me, and gratitude rose in my heart to God for granting me such a safe return to my *own dear home.*"

Thanksgiving Day itself broke gloriously sunlit. They went to church in the morning, of course, and heard what Emily thought was an excellent sermon. After a bountiful Thanksgiving dinner at home, the Dickinsons received callers. They had four different invitations for the evening and selected the two most promising. About seven o'clock all the Dickinsons and Emily Norcross, who had come home with her roommate for the holiday, went to Professor Warner's for a delightful visit with those old friends. Then the young people went on to Mrs. Samuel Mack's for a round of parlor games and what Emily called a "candy scrape." It was after ten o'clock before they returned home, and the day was not yet over.

The Honorable Edward Dickinson asked his college daughter to play and sing for him. Emily obliged with several songs, accompanying herself at the piano, and Squire Dickinson sat basking like any father in the accomplishments of his gifted daughter.

The next two days passed as happily, but Emily Dickinson was in tears again, and probably her mother and Lavinia too, when she climbed into the family carriage for the return trip to South Hadley. There would be no break at Christmas, a fast day and not a pagan holiday in Puritan New England. It was a solemn, churchgoing day, when any frivolity was frowned upon.

Emily Dickinson was studying chemistry and physiology now and was keenly interested in both. She kept protesting that she loved South Hadley Female Seminary, her dear new friends among the girls, and all her teachers, but there was a ring of dutifulness about her protestations. This term would be the longest one of the college year, and she admitted that she would not wish to live it over again. Already she was dreading the examinations at the end of it. Her father—it was encouragement and almost endearment from him—had urged her not to disgrace herself, and she was determined not to.

She was in the midst of studying the properties of sulfuric acid when a welcome letter came from Austin in mid-February 1848. She answered immediately, an indication of her loneliness. "Are you not gratified that I am so rapidly gaining correct ideas of female propriety and sedate deportment?" She supposed he had received a quantity of valentines. She had not received a single one but still hoped. Miss Lyon had forbidden her students to send any of what she called "those foolish notes," but the girls had surreptitiously dispatched about 150 of them.

Then Emily Dickinson grew more serious in the letter. She already knew that her father had decided not to send her back to Mount Holyoke for a second year, and her relief was boundless. She was almost in tears as she remembered "the blazing fire and the cheerful meal and the chair empty now I am gone," but her good angel reminded, her, " 'Only this year! only twenty-two weeks more, and then home again you shall stay.' "

Not only did time drag, there was also a larger fly in the ointment. It floundered, but only dug itself deeper, an old worry aggravated now by the insistence of Mary Lyon and her faculty.

Emily Dickinson was unregenerate. She had not been converted.

The academies—Andover, Exeter, Monson, Hopkins, Wilbraham, and all the others as well as Amherst—were hotbeds of revivalism. There were sporadic outbreaks of intense religious concern with ministers and missionaries exhorting to frenzy. The revival was as standard in the curricula of the New England colleges as rhetoric or moral philosophy.

Some of Emily's closest friends had been converted early at Amherst Academy and were blissfully certain of being in a state of grace, blessed on earth and assured of heaven. They worried that Emily had not seen the light, and Emily agonized with them. As did everyone except drunkards, criminals, and perhaps Indians, she believed that man is born in sin. Every man, woman, and child lived in sin until converted through an emotional awakening to dedication to God through Christ. Then, sins washed clean in the Blood of the Lamb, one was reborn. One was saved for life and for eternity.

Emily Dickinson yearned to be converted. She wished desperately to be saved. She thirsted for goodness on earth and hungered for happiness guaranteed through all eternity. The trouble was that she had not felt and did not feel the overwhelming religious emotion. She did not feel transported and reborn, and what she did not feel she could not pretend or avow.

In her bedrock honesty, which resembled her father's, Emily Dickinson was already Emily Dickinson. She had to be honest with others and even more demandingly so with herself. She had a clear mind. She could jest and mock. She could feel, feel almost too much too deeply. She could sing and play the piano. She had learned readily to act with "female propriety," but her essential honesty was impregnable. She could not help it any more than her father could help his unbending probity or her mother her gentleness. When it came to the things that mattered most to her, Emily Dickinson could never unbend either.

Mary Lyon begged her charges to repent, confess, and be saved. Most of them responded. Emily Dickinson could not. She was one of a small group of Mount Holyoke students who were "without hope" of grace. Her close friend in Amherst, Abby Wood, had been converted, and Emily thought that the resultant peace and happiness showed in Abby's face. Then Abiah Root felt the conviction that delivered her to God. Emily, who respected the actions of her friends and envied them the peace they had achieved, was alone. Devoutly, for she was devout, she wished it were otherwise, but it was not.

She was pulled too many ways by too many forces. She wished with all her heart to be at home, and at the same time she wished with all her heart to remain at Mount

Holyoke. She wished terribly to be converted, but she had to be her honest self. The result was that she fell ill, racked by a hard cough.

She tried to hide her illness from her family, but a friend who came to spend a week with her reported it, and Austin, now an Amherst sophomore, was promptly dispatched to bring her home. Emily demurred. She preferred to stay where she was, and her pride was involved. She did not wish all the old ladies in Amherst crying over her. Austin insisted. Emily cried. Austin was firm, and the defeated Emily was ingloriously carted home in the spring of 1848.

For about a month she was cared for there, sometimes a little too thoroughly for her comfort. "Father is quite a hand to give medicine, especially if it is not desirable to the patient," she wrote Abiah Root, partly in humor, partly in resentment, but she survived. She even studied and kept up with her classes and went on with her own reading: Longfellow's "Evangeline," Tennyson's "The Princess," and the didactic verse of the then popular Martin Tupper.

Early in May—more tears, but bird songs too—Emily Dickinson returned to Mount Holyoke. She was remorseful for time lost. Her conscience bothered her again that she had not used all of her time to best advantage, but, as she did all through her life, she found consolation in the spring.

While at home she had gone on several walking parties and found trailing arbutus, adder's-tongue, yellow violets, liverleaf, bloodroot, and other small flowers of the woods. She listed them all. In South Hadley, when tired with study, she walked beside the streams and went farther afield in search of wildflowers and calm.

5

When Edward Dickinson withdrew his older daughter from Mount Holyoke, he intended to keep her at home for a year, then send her to some other seminary. He never carried out the second part of his plan. Instead, Emily enrolled in Amherst Academy again for a post-graduate course in what for her was the best of all possible worlds.

She was home again with her family and friends, the visiting relatives, the public men who came to see her father. She had escaped the convent and the trance. She knew again from those who knew firsthand who was President and who might be. She had her books, her magazines, her newspaper. Her father, going back and forth to Boston, reported on what was happening or what he had made happen or what he was trying to make happen at the capital. She had her piano, her garden, her cooking. She knew what cases her father was trying in the court in Northampton and who was to marry whom and whether this boy was really attracted to that girl, or whether . . . Masculine profundities from her father and his friends, girlish chatter, parties, dances, berrying in summer, gathering chestnuts in fall, going to church or to town events in the First Church packed her days.

In First Church her father owned two of the white, high-backed pews, each with its door and latch, well to the front of what years later was to become College Hall. The church basement had been finished off for town meetings, agricultural fairs, court sessions, and various entertainments. A big stove in the vestibule, an innovation when Emily was three years old, heated the church. Long black stovepipes, running the length of the side aisles, warmed the congregation. There was no organ yet, but they had instrumental music, a bass viol having been introduced as early as 1817. Emily sat in the pew with her parents, sang from Dr. Watts's *Selected Hymns,* and knelt for prayer on one of the little carpeted crickets with which the pews were furnished.

The big bell of the First Church rang daily at noon. It rang again at nine o'clock in the evening to tell Amherst that it was time for all decent people to go to bed. Of the seventh generation of her family to worship in the town, Emily Dickinson knew the First Church, its ministers, the Old and New Testaments expounded—everything connected with orthodox Puritanism in New England—almost as well as she knew her own home and family.

She began to call herself "Emilie" and signed her letters so. Evidently the French spelling seemed more romantic to her than the pedestrian English. Probably it seemed to go better with the rapturous excitement that, part child, part woman—which she always remained—she found in life now.

She may never have become the belle she had envisioned, but she did not do badly. She was small, dainty, quick moving. She had had her daguerreotype taken when she was in South Hadley. Demure and serious, her dress simple, a narrow band of velvet about her neck secured by a brooch, she did not look like the vivacious young woman she was. The tintype showed her reddish hair parted severely in the middle and brushed close to her head, her eyes level and widely spaced, her lips firm. The family did not think it really looked like her. Emily

Fowler, granddaughter of Noah Webster (later Mrs. Gordon Ford of New York and the mother of historical novelist Paul Leicester Ford) and herself a beauty, says that Emily Dickinson had noticeable beauty in her lighted brown eyes and her shining auburn hair.

Certainly she was popular, the leader of a circle of lively young women who organized parties, poetry readings, and other happy frivolities. The academy had its school paper, handwritten and passed around, called *Forest Leaves*. Emily Dickinson was its humorist. According to Emily Fowler, what she wrote was instantly recognizable as hers, and irresistible. Certainly it was irresistible to the young editor of the Amherst College paper, who lifted and reprinted a prose valentine that she wrote. Thus Emily Dickinson achieved publication of a kind early in life and a little later, 1852, had her first poem published anonymously for a much wider audience in the *Springfield Daily Republican*. It was another valentine, *"Sic transit gloria mundi."*

In the richly intermixed activities of the First Church, Amherst College, private and public business, and the rather formal practices of upper-class Amherst society, the Dickinsons did things their way, and once they had done it, it was approved and became correct.

The story is probably untrue, for it was printed as an attack during the bitterness of a political campaign and vehemently denied, but it shows what some considered the Dickinson attitude to be.

Squire Dickinson was an active temperance man who at meetings in Amherst and Northampton advocated strict control over the sale of liquor. He was among the foremost of those who succeeded in getting a regulation passed that said that a purchaser had to have a doctor's order to buy medicinal whiskey. Yet he went to an apothecary's shop with a flask, which he ordered filled with brandy. When asked for his doctor's prescription, he said angrily, "Oh, that rule was not made for me!"

Despite his close association with it, Edward Dickinson did not join the First Church through confession of faith until January 6, 1856, when he was fifty-three years old. Evidently he had his reservations, and he did nothing unless he was thoroughly convinced. He could understand Emily's hesitation and did not press her to conversion. Edward Dickinson was consistently independent, and he was fair. He was just as consistent in assuming that the other members of his family had the same right to individuality as he asserted.

If the Dickinson family went its own way, each member of it went his own way as an independent human being. Mrs. Dickinson ran the big white house with hired help, had elaborate gardens, raised rare fruits, attended church almost all day on Sundays, and every year took charge of the elaborate preparations for the big Dickinson reception at which she reigned as hostess. Austin and Lavinia had their own friends and activities. Emily Dickinson was as strongly marked as her father and in her own way as imperious. It is the similarity in their characters rather than the often emphasized difference that is most striking. Though the girls sometimes did not return from sleighing parties and the like until the early hours of the morning, he seems not to have objected or to have interfered with their riding or going to parties with a succession of college tutors and seniors. Edward Dickinson was stern and stubborn, but he was just and must have been more understanding than he allowed his usual manner to indicate. Had her father not had these basic qualities, the life that

Emily Dickinson later elected to lead would have been impossible.

All of the Dickinson children had a way with words. Lavinia became notorious for her virulence in speech and the sharp phrases often meant to shock. Austin was readily articulate and, when he was not writing his father letters that were all business, showed humor and a deftness for breezy phrases in his letters. Words were Edward Dickinson's business, in his briefs, in his pleadings, and in his legislative activities, and he could express himself pungently in his letters. The humorist of *Forest Leaves* came honestly by the talent she was to perfect in her poetry.

After his graduation from Amherst College in 1850, Austin Dickinson went to Boston to teach in the Endicott School. A year later he entered Harvard Law School. Intelligent and personable, with the same rich auburn hair as his sister, Austin was as upright as his father but had the softening of his mother's less rigid character. Austin was sorely missed at home, especially by Emily, who tried to keep him close through frequent letters bursting with family news, village gossip, her feelings. . . .

Why hadn't he written? The weather had been hot and dry. In a letter of 1851 she jested merrily but added, "If I hadn't been afraid you would 'poke fun' at my feelings, I had written a sincere letter, but since 'the world is hollow, and dollie's stuffed with sawdust' I really do not think we had better expose our feelings."

In July of that year she wrote Austin at length about a great event. The family had driven to Northampton to hear Jenny Lind sing in the Edwards church. First, one of their horses had reared and balked so badly that they had to procure a different one. Then a thunderstorm broke and the rain fell in torrents. Finally they got there. ". . .

how Jennie came out like a child and sang and sang again —how bouquets fell in showers, and the roof was rent with applause—how it thundered outside, and inside with the thunder of God and men—judge ye which was the loudest —how we all loved Jennie Lind, but not accustomed oft to her manner of singing didn't fancy *that* so well as we did *her*."

Jenny Lind was good, but their father put on a better show. "Father sat all evening looking *mad,* and yet so much amused you would have *died* a-laughing. . . . It wasn't sarcasm exactly, nor it wasn't disdain, it was infinitely funnier than either of those virtues, as if old Abraham had come to see the show, and thought it was all very well, but a little excess of *monkey!*"

Another day their mother was lying down, suffering badly with neuralgia, which drove Emily to household tasks she detested. That was material good enough for a letter to Abiah Root, but it was of their father that she wrote most often to Austin. Once it was Lavinia who gave Austin the latest news of him. "Oh! dear! Father is killing the horse. I wish you'd come quick if you want to see him alive. He is whipping him because he did'nt [sic] look quite 'umble enough this morning. Oh! Austin, it makes me angry to see that 'noble [sic] creature so abused. Emilie is screaming at the top of her voice. She's so vexed about it."

Father usually got his own way with man or horse, but not always. At one time he became so annoyed with the minister that on Sunday he stayed home from church and allowed neither of his daughters to attend any of the services. His wife, who had more spirit than she often is credited with, went despite his disapproval.

Father dominates the letters. Emily and Austin loved

him, knew him, could never forget him for long. He was news. Emily opened a long letter of October 1851 with this colorful description:

> ... The breakfast is so warm, and pussy is here a-singing, and the tea-kettle sings too, as if to see which was loudest, and I am afraid lest kitty should be beaten—yet a shadow falls upon my morning picture—where is the youth so bold, the bravest of our fold—a seat is empty here—spectres sit in your chair, and now and then nudge father with their long, bony elbows. ...

In another letter Emily told Austin, "Father is as uneasy when you are gone away as if you catch a trout and put him in Sahara." March 18, 1853, she wrote Austin that his letters were very funny. They were about the only jokes they had now he was gone.

> Father takes great delight in your remarks to him—puts on his spectacles and reads them o'er and o'er as if it was a blessing to have an only son. He reads all the letters you write, as soon as he gets them at the post-office, no matter to whom addressed; then he makes me read them aloud at the supper-table again. ... I believe at this moment, Austin, that there's nobody living for whom Father has such respect as for you.

She wrote Austin in one letter that he was funnier than Punch—much funnier—but sometimes Father did not get the point. One letter confused even Emily. What did Austin mean? "Father . . . looked very much confused, and finally put on his spectacles, which didn't seem to help him much—I don't think a telescope would have assisted him."

Emily Dickinson's letters to the absent Austin are vivid, fond, and perceptive. Obviously she enjoyed writing them. She enjoyed any writing, and their father was an inescapable subject. One Sunday they missed Austin more than ever after a visit home the week before. It was November and cold. The snow was crusted on the Pelham Hills. The family had just come home from meeting. "Father and mother sit in state in the sitting room perusing such papers, only, as they are well assured, have nothing carnal in them. Vinnie is eating an apple." It was not that their parents would not read worldly books and periodicals, but that they would not read them on Sunday. Eating an apple was permissible any day.

Father had decided ideas, though, on what was and what was not worth reading. He took Emily to task for wasting her time on *Uncle Tom's Cabin* when it was published in 1852. He also said that Charles Dickens and the rest were as nothing compared to books written when he was a boy. He was particularly scornful of "somebody's reveries." This was Ik Marvel's (Donald G. Mitchell) *Reveries of a Bachelor,* sentimental musings which Emily Dickinson and her young contemporaries adored. A friend of Professor L. Clark Seelye, Mitchell was a frequent visitor to Amherst.

Edward Dickinson had worked hard in Boston and all over the state to bring the railroad to Amherst. His efforts succeeded. Amherst, Sunderland, and Montague were to be joined via Belchertown with New London, Connecticut. Naturally he was "really sober from excessive satisfaction." Naturally, too, he was marshal of a great day of celebration when the first train went out in 1853. He "went marching around with New London at his heels like some old Roman general on a triumph day." Father was funny, but he was wonderful and even to his daughter not always predictable.

Monday evening we were all startled by a violent church-bell ringing and thinking of nothing but fire, rushed out in the street to see. The sky was a beautiful red, bordering on a crimson, and rays of a gold pink color were constantly shooting off from a kind of sun in the centre. People were alarmed by this beautiful phenomenon, supposing that fires somewhere were coloring the sky. The exhibition lasted for nearly fifteen minutes, and the streets were full of people wondering and admiring. Father happened to see it among the very first, and rang the bell himself to call attention to it.

Who but the Squire would have dared ring the big bell of the Baptist church, which Emily Dickinson was sure would ring in the Day of Judgment? Edward Dickinson was not unimaginative. Here was something beautiful, perhaps portentous. He wanted Amherst to see the aurora borealis. Perhaps he had always wanted to ring the big bell, and his iron control gave way for a moment to adequate excuse.

The tone of a letter that Emily Dickinson wrote Austin on Easter evening, March 27, 1853, was characteristically flippant and lighthearted, but the letter carried a revealing threat. Evidently Austin had essayed a poem.

Now, Brother Pegasus, I'll tell you what it is—I've been in the habit *myself* of writing some few things, and it rather appears to me that you're getting away with my patent, so you'd better be somewhat careful or I'll call the police.

Later, Emily was to say that she had written no poetry

before her thirtieth year. Perhaps it was not what she considered poetry, but she had written a rhymed valentine to Elbridge G. Bowdoin, then a young law student in her father's office, in 1850. She wrote another to William Howland, also one of her father's students, in 1852. That was the verse that was published when Howland sent it to the *Republican*. Now, with the encouragement of Benjamin Newton, she was writing more verse.

Born in Worcester in 1821, thus nine years older than Emily, Benjamin Franklin Newton came to Amherst in the winter of 1847–1848 to study law in the offices of Dickinson & Bowdoin. A Unitarian, more liberal in his thinking than Edward Dickinson might have wished, he was bright and promising, with marked literary tastes. He became another of the young men who were welcome guests in the Dickinson home. Seemingly he singled Emily out for his attention, or she singled him out. He became "a beautiful new friend." They talked of books and poetry. He introduced her to writing he treasured, particularly the poetry of Ralph Waldo Emerson, which had just been published. Emily showed him some of her early attempts at verse, and he told her he thought she could be a poet. This was no parlor praise. It was the considered opinion of one she knew to be a discerning critic. Emily thrilled to his words and was intoxicated with hope.

After two years Newton returned to Worcester for further study of the law. He was admitted to the bar and began successful practice in his native city, becoming State's attorney for Worcester County. He and Emily Dickinson corresponded regularly. Then in 1853, when he was already very ill, he married a woman twelve years older than he. He wrote Emily Dickinson in March speaking of his possible death. Aged thirty-three, he died before the month was out.

As she had been when Leonard Humphrey died, Emily Dickinson was stricken, but this time it was worse. She had known Humphrey as a loved teacher. Her relationship with Newton, whatever it was, had been closer, and she was older. Anxiously she wrote Newton's Unitarian minister, the Reverend Edward Everett Hale (author in 1863 of *The Man Without a Country*), asking whether Newton had died in grace. She explained her concern. "Mr. Newton became to me a gentle, yet grave Preceptor, teaching me what to read, what authors to admire, what was most grand or beautiful in nature, and that sublime lesson, a faith in things unseen, and in life again, much nobler and much more blessed."

Emily Dickinson never forgot Benjamin Franklin Newton or her debt to him.

Another friendship into which Emily leaped at this time was far different from her relationship with Newton, and its effects lasted the rest of her life. Susan Gilbert, the daughter of a tavern keeper in Deerfield, was brought to Amherst as a small child when her father leased the Mansion House. The youngest of seven children, she was left an orphan at eleven. She lived first with an aunt in Geneva, New York, then came back to live with an older married sister in Amherst. Thus it was not until Emily Dickinson and Susan Gilbert were both sixteen that the girls met as students at Amherst Academy, and not until after Emily's return from Mount Holyoke that their friendship developed.

Susan Gilbert fascinated Emily Dickinson. She was pretty, talkative, and colorful, and she knew her way around. Supported in part by an older brother who lived in Michigan, she had traveled and at an early age learned how to handle people to get what she wanted. Susan Gilbert possessed charm and social grace, mingled with astuteness and strong ambition. There was nothing of the little girl in this young woman.

Emily took to Sue with abandon. Sue was everything that was wonderful. She gushed over her. It is one of the anomalies of Emily's strong clear-eyed vision and independent spirit that throughout life she could gush with extravagant sentimentality. She wanted to keep wonderful Sue forever, and there was one way of ensuring at least an approximation of possession. That was through her brother Austin. Soon, with the help of Lavinia, Emily Dickinson was matchmaking as if born to the trade.

Emily Dickinson's letters to Austin, especially during 1853, were packed with allusions to Sue, most of them ecstatic. Sue had been at the house or they had been to see Sue. They shared Austin's treasured letters with Sue. Sue was there when one of his letters came, and they read it together. May 17, 1853, Emily wrote, as she so often did, of her own loneliness, but spent most of her time talking of Sue. Later, June 13, 1853, Emily was happy because they were at Sue's house or Sue was at their house all the time. A week later the Dickinson home was crowded for commencement with all kinds of people, some, as Emily described them, "the poor in this world's goods" and others representatives of "the almighty dollar." She did not know what in the world they were all after. She wished she, Lavinia, and Sue could escape into some vast wilderness until noisy commencement week was over.

November 8, 1853, was very cold. The squash had to be moved. Emily got in all her flowers. Father, who had been in Springfield overnight on business, had got home before they expected him, just in time for dinner. Emily was lonely.

A little later Vinnie enclosed a note with one of Emily's

letters. The dining room had been closed for the winter and the table moved into the sitting room, she said. She had been reading aloud to Father, who had "condescended to spend the evening with them *socially*." Vinnie underlined the word. "I think Father is perfectly home sick without you. What will he do when we are *all* gone?" she wondered, for by this time Austin and Susan Gilbert were engaged.

Innocently, Vinnie assumed that she and Emily too would marry and have homes and children of their own.

6

In the idiom of her niece and biographer, Martha Dickinson Bianchi, Emily Dickinson had at about this time "a spicy affair" with a young law student in her father's office. Who? Howland? Bowdoin? Presumably Madame Bianchi meant Newton, but she does not say. Perhaps she hinted correctly, perhaps not.

Emily Dickinson was attracted to men, particularly older men. Those she came to know best she met in her own home. They were friends and associates of her father, men of stature and accomplishment, formidable men. The young men pleased her well enough—she sparkled for them, danced with them, went driving with them, sent them valentines—but her father and his chosen associates were reality.

These men were strength and security in a spinning world, and instinctively she trusted them. She depended upon her father and men of his generation more than upon her own judgment or the minds and emotions of friends her own age. It was part of the childlike quality she maintained throughout her precocious youth and then her actual maturity. Neither as a young woman nor as an older one did she ever become a poet aloof from the world about her. She had read the newspapers and magazines from childhood. At home she had listened gravely to debates on the public considerations of the day. She knew what was going on and learned much of what she knew at home.

Clients, college officials, and fellow trustees were routine visitors in the Dickinson household. As she had indicated in one of the letters to Austin, so were petty influence-seekers, pompous rich men, and fawning poor men. Edward Dickinson was an astute politician. Those who are not astute do not get elected. He knew how to get what he wanted in the political world.

Politicians cannot function without the press, and one of those closest to Edward Dickinson and frequently a guest in his home did not just represent the power of the press in New England and even nationally. In western Massachusetts, he *was* the press.

The first Samuel Bowles came up the Connecticut River from Hartford with a wife, a baby, and a hand printing press. In September 1824 he founded the *Springfield Republican*. A year and a half later the second Samuel Bowles was born, February 9, 1826. Thus he was not quite five years older than Emily Dickinson. Chronologically he was closer to her generation than to her father's, but in accomplishment, influence, and power he ranked with the older man.

Young Bowles joined his father's *Republican* when he was seventeen. Running errands and covering local news hardly satisfied his driving ambition. He persuaded his father to issue a daily as well as a weekly edition. He fought and vanquished rival newspapers, developed thorough coverage of the towns and villages of the Connecticut Valley through a string of correspondents, and covered important events and personages himself. Young Bowles worked so hard building the *Republican* into a unique newspaper that he early suffered the first of a series of nervous and physical breakdowns and was sent to Louisiana in the winter of 1844–1845 to recover.

He returned to work even harder. Doing much of his

own reporting, he packed the *Republican* with local intelligence and gossip, ran a weekly religious column, featured human-interest stories, and, quick to use the telegraph for national news, made his paper a powerful engine of the Whig Party.

Tall, somewhat stooped, hawk-nosed, with penetrating eyes, Samuel Bowles II was a hard taskmaster at the office. Socially he was witty, charming, a favorite dinner-table companion. Taking over complete control of the *Republican* on the death of his father in 1851, he made it what the redoubtable Horace Greeley called the best provincial newspaper in the country.

In western Massachusetts there were the Bible and the *Springfield Republican,* and people trusted the second almost as much as the first. If the *Republican* said it, it was true. If Sam Bowles and the *Republican* backed it, it was right whatever it was. Bowles made only one bad mistake, but his readers rectified it in their own way. He began to publish a Sunday edition. The orthodox saw this as wicked. At first they refused the Sunday *Republican,* but they learned how to deal with it. Fearful of missing news, gossip, or religious intelligence of importance, they took the paper but did not read it or pay for it until the next day.

Emily Dickinson knew and read the *Republican* from childhood. She knew its forceful and romantic-looking editor as a charming guest, an important man of the great world, a staunch supporter of her father, and a friend to them all.

Allied with Bowles was a gentler figure who also frequented the Dickinson home. Dr. Josiah Gilbert Holland had earned his title honestly. Born in Belchertown in

1817, he attended Northampton High School for a time, and graduated from the Berkshire Medical College in 1844. He tried but failed to establish a medical practice in Springfield, where he met and married Elizabeth Chapin, descendant of one of the city's founders. In 1848, when Emily Dickinson was still at Mount Holyoke, Holland abandoned medicine and went south to teach school in Richmond, Virginia, then in Vicksburg, Mississippi. In 1850 he returned to Springfield and to work for which he proved to be eminently suited.

He joined Samuel Bowles on the *Republican* to write human-interest stories while Bowles concentrated on public affairs. It was a happy combination. Many of Holland's contributions were magazinelike rather than reportorial. He began with a series of imaginary letters from "Max Mannering" to a sister in the country. He wrote, and the *Republican* published serially, a long history of western Massachusetts, which is still a valuable source. His whimsical "Timothy Titcomb" letters, which appeared first in the *Republican,* were published in 1858 as a book, entitled *Titcomb's Letters to Young People, Single and Married.* Holland was to become a far traveler and a prolific writer. His wife became one of Emily Dickinson's favorite correspondents to the end of her life.

Bowles and Holland were her father's friends. She might jest that Father walked like Cromwell when he brought in wood for the kitchen fire. She laughed when he agreed with visiting Monson relatives that all young men who smoked should catch fire, dared observe that it would be quite a conflagration, and was properly squelched, but she never doubted his authority or his love. She remembered that when she was a small child and had suffered some hurt or dismay, it was to him, not to her mother, that she had run for comfort and healing.

That Bowles and Holland were her father's friends was enough, but they were also writers, and she wanted achingly to write. She could follow their work in the *Republican,* then know them in the flesh at her father's dinner table. They liked her, and she knew they liked her. They delighted in her wit and perceptiveness, which were like their own. Bowles and Holland became and remained permanent forces in the life of Emily Dickinson.

There was one other who stood out among the public men who were welcomed in the Dickinson home. Born in Ipswich, Massachusetts, of an old colonial family, Otis Phillips Lord was somewhat older than Bowles and Holland, eighteen years older than Emily. A brilliant lawyer, a successful politician, another strong Whig, he also was a magnetic figure.

Lord had graduated from Amherst College in 1832. He read law in Springfield, took his law degree at Harvard in 1836, and began to practice in Ipswich. October 9, 1843, when Emily Dickinson was twelve years old, he married Elizabeth Wise Farley. The next year they moved to Salem, and it was from there that Lord was elected to the state legislature where, with Edward Dickinson, he served first in the House, then in the Senate. Eloquent, readily articulate, a dynamic courtroom pleader, Otis Lord was twice defeated for the speakership of the Massachusetts House but was successful in 1854. Twice he was nominated for the United States Congress, and twice he lost, but the faithful Whig Party man got his political reward in 1859, when he was appointed to the Massa-chusetts Superior Court.

Emily's father, Samuel Bowles, Dr. Holland, Judge Lord —these were men of thought and action. Others could read in their newspapers, magazines, and books what they said and did. Emily Dickinson knew them intimately in the privacy of her home. She never had to hitch a wagon to some distant star. Hers was a polished and delicately upholstered Dickinson cabriolet to begin with. Neither these men nor her younger friends knew that it was really a chariot. Perhaps Emily Dickinson herself did not know, but she did know that Pegasus was a faster horse than even her father or Deacon Sweetser drove.

Bowles, Holland, Lord, and a score of others were too busy anyway to worry much about horses, either four-legged or four-legged and winged. They were planning and plotting and bending all their efforts toward an ambitious and practical end.

In June 1852 Edward Dickinson was a delegate to the Whig convention in Baltimore. The convention nominated General Winfield Scott for President, but Edward Dickinson backed Daniel Webster ballot after ballot to the end. By September, Edward Dickinson was standing for the Whig nomination for Congress.

The *Hampshire and Franklin Express* backed him enthusiastically. In a September 10 editorial it said of him, "A true Whig in every sense of the word, he is ever ready to sacrifice personal preference to the good of principle. . . . He is no trimmer, courting the breezes of popularity first upon one tack and then upon another, but straight forward, steadfast and reliable."

On September 13, after two ballots, Edward Dickinson

was the unanimous choice of the Tenth District convention in Northampton. His acceptance speech was characteristic. He had made no campaign promises. He made no promises now. "In thus accepting the nomination, I can give no assurance of fidelity in the discharge of the duties of the office of representative, if elected, beyond what is furnished by my past life."

Sam Bowles and the *Republican* backed Edward Dickinson to the hilt. The *Hampshire Gazette* supported him. Austin Dickinson wrote his friends soliciting their votes for his father. Edward Dickinson urged fellow Whig politicians to get out the vote. In an election-day editorial Samuel Bowles wrote, "Let every Whig come out to-day and give his vote to Edward Dickinson of Amherst, for member of Congress. . . . He is a man upon whose name rests no stain—a firm, straight Whig, a pure citizen, and a thoroughly capable, honest man who has never begged and bargained for votes. . . ."

Edward Dickinson was elected to the House of Representatives in Washington by a large plurality, and Amherst celebrated his victory with a huge bonfire. Asked the next morning how he liked it, the Squire remarked dryly that his woodpile had shrunk noticeably overnight.

7

Exciting years were coming up for Emily Elizabeth Dickinson.

Her father was a congressman, excitement enough for any young girl. The Honorable Edward Dickinson ruled town and college, the Cattle Show, the temperance movement in Hampshire County, and a half-dozen committees and commissions. He had helped run the Commonwealth. Now he was helping to run the nation.

Early in 1854 Mrs. Dickinson and Lavinia went to Washington to see him doing it. After stopping at the Astor House in New York on the way south, they went to Willard's Hotel in Washington, already famous as a political gathering place and haunt of Washington society. Representative Dickinson was soon busy with congressional affairs and in Whig politics. His wife and daughter mingled with the families of other statesmen at Willard's, where Vinnie is said to have become the center of an admiring group. She was pretty, flirtatious, and, above all, sharp-tongued.

The following spring the whole Dickinson family went to Washington. There a flurry of preparation, the girls getting all kinds of finery for the anticipated season. Emily Dickinson said she would probably look like an embarrassed peacock unused to his plumage. Again the Astor House, then Willard's.

Passage of the Kansas-Nebraska Bill, a compromise allowing the extension of slavery, had been a defeat for the Whigs and another indication of the dissolution of the party. At a meeting in the rooms of the Honorable Edward Dickinson and the Honorable Thomas D. Eliot of Massachusetts some twenty members of the House decided that the Whigs' only hope lay in forming a new party, to be called the Republican Party. Thus Edward Dickinson was one of the founders of the party that would elect Abraham Lincoln to the Presidency in 1860. In late January 1855, however, he was busy petitioning Congress to raise the salaries of civilian employees in the United States arsenal at Springfield.

At the same time he was proud to show off his wife and his two attractive daughters, one with quick eyes that almost matched her auburn hair. Lavinia and Emily Dickinson joined the parade of fashion in the Willard's lobby. They met famous men. They ate formal dinners and attended formal receptions. According to Madame Bianchi, Emily astounded her father's colleagues with her wit and insight into public questions, and she shocked the Chief Justice of the Supreme Court. When at one dinner the brandy was set afire and the plum pudding brought in enveloped in blue flames, she asked innocently, "Oh, sir, may one eat of hellfire with impunity here?"

Mrs. Dickinson and Austin seem to have left for home after about two weeks in the capital. Emily and Vinnie stayed on, delighting in the beauty of early spring in the District of Columbia. A month after their arrival the maples were in leaf and the grass was green in sunny places while, they knew, all was still ice and snow in Amherst. Emily exclaimed over "the pomp—the court—the etiquette" in a letter to Susan and Martha Gilbert, though, characteristically, she said those things were all as nothing compared to her love for them. She marveled at all the elegance and grandeur, particularly at the diamonds worn by the ornately gowned women of the capital.

A congressman from Alabama and his wife were staying at Willard's too. Mrs. James Brown gave the Dickinson girls a copy of *The Last Leaf from Sunny Side* by the popular religious and sentimental novelist Elizabeth Stuart Phelps. The great Abolitionist senator from Massachusetts, Charles Sumner, gave the congressman from Amherst a copy of a new book by L. Maria Child for his wife.

Emily and Lavinia saw all the sights of the city, but it was one outside the District that most impressed the emotional Emily. "One soft spring day we glided down the Potomac in a painted boat to Mount Vernon," she wrote Elizabeth Chapin Holland. They visited the marble tomb, then went on to the house. It thrilled her to lift the same latch that George Washington had raised when he last came home. All her life she liked to remember the great of the world, note their birthdays, and remember their deeds.

Even after their protracted stay in Washington the sisters did not return immediately to Amherst. They stopped off in Philadelphia for several more weeks, staying in that city with a school friend, Eliza Coleman. Her father, the Reverend Lyman Coleman, had been a principal of Amherst Academy.

It has been assumed and reassumed a score of times that it was on this visit that Emily Dickinson meet the Reverend Charles Wadsworth, pastor of the Arch Street Presbyterian church in Philadelphia. Wadsworth, forty-one, married, with several children, was one of the celebrated preachers of the day, often compared to Henry Ward Beecher of Brooklyn.

Wadsworth was a compelling pulpit orator. Visitors

were taken to hear him as naturally as visitors were shown Mount Vernon in Washington or Mount Auburn Cemetery in Cambridge. Dark-haired and dark-eyed, the slender Wadsworth looked like one of the ancient Hebrew prophets. His delivery was made hypnotic by bold gestures and an actor's caressing voice that he could make tremulous with emotion. Crowds flocked to get seats or standing room in his church. On New Year's Day 1851 a group of admiring Philadelphians presented him with an ornate casket overflowing with five-dollar gold pieces.

So much has been made of the supposed meeting of Emily Dickinson and Charles Wadsworth at this time that it has become the central part of the Dickinson legend. Emily Dickinson revered Wadsworth. She wrote to him for years. She asked his spiritual advice. She treasured a volume of his privately printed sermons. Twice he came to see her in Amherst. Whether or not he was the object of her tempestuous love and matchless love poetry no one knows, but the melodrama in the possibility has proved irresistible to a number of the poet's biographers.

Certainly Emily Dickinson returned to Amherst stimulated by travel, new people, and a thousand new impressions, and soon there was new excitement. In April 1853 the Honorable Edward Dickinson purchased from Samuel S. Mack, son of General Mack, the mansion on East Main Street that Samuel Fowler Dickinson had built. He paid six thousand dollars for it and spent almost as much as that repairing and enlarging it. The family moved back into the ancestral home in which Emily Dickinson had been born and in which she would spend the rest of her life.

She told Mrs. Holland of the move in one of the most brilliant of her brilliant letters, a letter so grave and gay, so humorous and sober, that she signed it accurately "from your mad Emilie."

> I cannot tell you how we moved. I had rather not remember. I believe "my effects" were brought in a bandbox, and the "deathless me" on foot, not many moments after. I took at the time a memorandum of my several senses, and also of my hat and coat and my best shoes—but it was lost in the melee, and I am out with a lantern looking for myself. . . .
>
> . . . I often wish I was a grass, or a toddling daisy, whom all these problems of the dust might not terrify—and should my own machinery get slightly out of gear *please,* kind ladies and gentlemen, some one stop the wheel. . . .

The move was too much for Mrs. Dickinson. For a considerable time she suffered severe nervous strain and was forced to spend her days in bed or in an easy chair. Emily and Vinnie did their best to get settled in what for Emily still did not seem like home. The Pleasant Street house was put up for sale and purchased by the college for a faculty house.

The Dickinsons now had one new home. Little more than a year later there were two large Dickinson houses on the ample estate.

William Austin Dickinson and Susan Gilbert had been engaged for more than two years. Austin was Amherst's most eligible bachelor, the town catch. Susan Gilbert was pretty, lively, and self-assured. They made a colorful couple. Yet there were many who felt that the marriage of a Dickinson to the orphaned daughter of a bibulous tavern keeper was not quite the thing. There was unfriendly gossip, which Emily Dickinson loyally advised Sue to ignore.

She had pushed the engagement with every strategem she could use. Emily Dickinson's enthusiasms were never moderate. Sometimes, though, they waned as fast as they waxed. She and Sue were still close, but they were not the soul sisters she had once imagined. Neither slow nor stupid, Emily Dickinson must have quickly become aware of that.

Something more than a spat between friends must have caused a serious rift between the two young women in 1854, for in the early fall Emily Dickinson wrote Susan Gilbert a coldly incisive note in which she said that lately they had disagreed so often—about what, she did not say—that Susan could take her choice about continuing or severing their intimacy. Very clearly Emily Dickinson made it plain that it was a matter of complete indifference to her. She had suffered loss before and then found that what she had lost had lacked the value she had attached to it.

This is hard Edward Dickinson language, and there is a finality about the dismissal. Yet, once Austin had been convinced, Susan Gilbert continued to be his choice. If only for appearance's sake, she would remain dear to Emily Dickinson.

Susan Huntington Gilbert and William Austin Dickinson were married in the home of the bride's aunt in Geneva, New York, July 1, 1856. The ceremony was performed by the Reverend Joseph Haven, professor of mental and moral philosophy at Amherst College. Thus the marriage had Amherst's blessing, but it is not on record that any of the Dickinsons attended the wedding. They awaited their son and brother and his bride at home.

This break was the first in the tightly knit family. The first loss and the first admission of an outsider, it was more decisive for Austin than marriage ordinarily is for a groom.

Four years of metropolitan Boston and a Harvard Law degree behind him, Austin had been looking for fresh fields to conquer. He decided to go west, where he and Sue could grow with a new and expanding country, and he spent a month of the winter before his marriage in Chicago seeking out opportunities.

Edward Dickinson had other ideas. He prized his son and did not like the prospect of his being a thousand miles beyond the reach of his advice and help. Like his children, Edward Dickinson could easily be two things at once, and here he was both selfish and handsomely generous.

He offered to build Austin and Sue a fine home on land next to his own and to take Austin into his law firm as an equal partner and to make him heir apparent to the business as well as to the Dickinson estates. Undoubtedly Sue was eager to accept, and Austin relinquished his dreams for a golden actuality.

Edward Dickinson did one more thing to help his son get started. The Squire bought two Bibles, one for himself and one for Austin.

The splendid new house was built on ample grounds adjoining the Dickinson property to the west, and Austin Dickinson began the long career in which he finally would succeed his father in the social, legal, college, and church hierarchy of Amherst.

At first there was much running back and forth between the two houses. Night after night Emily went across the broad lawn and through the hedge, carrying a lantern and accompanied by her big dog and constant companion, Carlo. They talked and laughed at Austin's. They played games. Emily improvised wildly on the piano for hours at a time, something she also liked to do at home, frequently in the middle of the night, when her imagination and her fingers raced free in the silence and the darkness. Sometimes Edward Dickinson had to go over to the new house after midnight to bring his reluctant daughter home.

Something else had Emily Dickinson excited and elated. She was really writing poetry now. She dared tell Austin and Sue that she hoped to make them proud of her someday—a long way off, she added. In a letter to Louise Norcross, her Boston cousin, she reminded her that once when their families were out driving and they were alone in the dining room they had decided to be distinguished. In her own mind, central purpose hardening, Emily Dickinson was beginning to think she could make her girlish decision come true.

8

The crux of the Emily Dickinson mystery comes here—or somewhere in these years. No one knows the sequence of events or their coincidence. Emily Dickinson fell in love, and she was disappointed in love.

The story was long current in Amherst that she fell in love with someone of whom her father disapproved. He forbade her to see the man again. Thereupon Emily Dickinson vowed never to leave her father's house and grounds again, and she never did willingly.

In *This Was a Poet* George Whicher hazarded a guess that if there was any basis to the rumor, the suitor may have been Benjamin Franklin Newton. He was poor and seemingly without prospects. He was a Unitarian, thus godless in the eyes of the orthodox. Physically frail, he early showed signs of the tuberculosis that finally caused his death.

There are many versions of this story. Ebenezer Porter Dickinson, who retired as reference librarian in 1968 after fifty years in the Amherst College library, knew a different one from his mother. Emily Dickinson was spending too much time with the family's handsome young Irish gardener. She seemed enamored. Her father sternly ordered her to cease and desist. His fiery daughter then vowed, etc., etc.

Intent on romanticizing her famous aunt, Madame Bianchi says in her *Life and Letters of Emily Dickinson* that it was on the visit to Philadelphia that Emily Dickinson met "the fate she had instinctively shunned." She fell in love with a married man. He pursued her to Amherst. According to Madame Bianchi, Lavinia came running across the lawn to Susan Dickinson one day and gasped, "That man is here and Mother and Father are away and I'm afraid Emily will go with him!" The niece makes the story even more mysterious by saying that Emily Dickinson told the awful truth to no one but her mother, who guarded the secret to her grave.

Whicher plumped for the Philadelphia story, repeated so many times since, but named the man as the Reverend Charles Wadsworth. Twice, Wadsworth came to Amherst to see Emily Dickinson. They corresponded until his death. She called him her spiritual adviser.

Susceptible women did fall in love with spellbinding ministers and did, though often only in fantasy, carry on romances with them. In the nineteenth century such men were as famous as television personalities, athletic figures, actors, or politicians are today. Not only were they headlined heroes, but they were also surrounded by enticing mystery. They knew all the secrets of life and death. They were privy to the esoteric meanings of baptism, communion, and salvation, as familiar with things unseen as with things temporal.

Emily Dickinson, who doubted only the trappings and never the truths of orthodox Christianity as she understood it and who lived all her life in the vocabulary of evangelical Protestantism, would have been more susceptible than most.

That she was romantically in love with the Reverend Charles Wadsworth seems improbable. That he responded in kind seems impossible. Yet he became and remained an important figure in her life.

Wadsworth called on Emily in the spring of 1861. In

December of that year he accepted a call to the Calvary Church in San Francisco and went there with his wife and children. It has been conjectured that Emily Dickinson referred to him and to this move when she said, ". . . he was not contented I be his scholar, so he left the land." In 1870 he returned to a different church in Philadelphia. Ten years later he called again on the woman who by calling herself "Empress of Calvary" had lent credence to the credulous in suspecting the preacher.

In the introduction to his three-volume variorum edition of Emily Dickinson's poetry, 1951, Thomas H. Johnson followed Whicher in supporting the candidacy of Wadsworth. He developed the theory further in his *Emily Dickinson, an Interpretive Biography,* in 1963.

In 1930 Josephine Pollitt proved to her own satisfaction and presumably the satisfaction of those who read her *Emily Dickinson, the Human Background of Her Poetry* that the man in the poet's life was really Major Edward Bissell Hunt, first husband of Emily's schoolgirl friend, Helen Maria Fiske. The trouble with this story is that the army engineer thought Emily Dickinson "uncanny" and said so.

It was not the gallant soldier at all. According to Genevieve Taggard in 1930 (*The Life and Mind of Emily Dickinson*), Emily was in love with George Gould, a distant cousin and penniless Amherst student. He was the hero and Emily the heroine of the garden scene in which Edward Dickinson banished the impetuous suitor and his daughter renounced love and all the world.

While an undergraduate Gould had invited Emily Dickinson to a candy pull at the Montagues', and she kept his invitation always, writing one of her poems on the back of it as late as 1876. Gould was the editor of the

Amherst College *Indicator* who published the humorous valentine Emily Dickinson sent him in 1850. After he graduated he sent her long letters from Andover Theological Seminary and then from Union Theological Seminary, where he was a divinity student. He wrote her more letters from the Far West, where he went railroad engineering in search of health, then from Europe when he traveled there with John Bartholomew Gough, a reformed drunkard who became a dramatic temperance lecturer. Gould finally became a well-known minister in Worcester. After Emily Dickinson's death he admitted that he had kept her letters hidden in a small trunk for many years but said that the trunk had been lost.

Of course, it was not really the Reverend George Gould either. Emily Dickinson was in love with Samuel Bowles. All of her most outspoken and almost violent poems of a star-crossed lover and a woman forced to forgo her love because the man is unattainable, or far away, or sometimes near death, were about Samuel Bowles. At least that is the thesis proposed—with plausible evidence from her letters—by David Higgins in a 1967 study out of Rutgers University. According to Higgins, Austin Dickinson said that his sister loved Samuel Bowles "beyond sentimentality"—which can mean as much or as little as you please.

If it was not Samuel Bowles, it was Dr. Josiah Gilbert Holland. When Mabel Loomis Todd came to Amherst in 1881, she heard it hinted that Emily Dickinson and Dr. Holland had been in love but that Squire Dickinson, who saw nothing remarkable in the rising journalist, had forbidden their marriage. The brilliant young woman, who became Emily's friend and her first posthumous editor, noted in her journal that the story was not unlikely because Dr. Holland had long been an intimate friend of the Dickinson family.

In her forties Emily Dickinson was openly in love with Otis Phillips Lord and after the death of his first wife may have hoped to marry him. Lord seems to have returned her love, but unless she fell in love with him earlier, and, in her eyes and the eyes of the world she knew, guiltily, it does not explain her tempestuous poetry about love found but quickly lost, which she wrote years before that.

There are four possibilities:

1. Emily Dickinson was in love with Leonard Humphrey, George Gould, Benjamin Franklin Newton, Charles Wadsworth, Samuel Bowles, Josiah Holland, the handsome Irish gardener, or Otis Lord.

2. She was in love at various times with one or two or three of them, actually or in her fired imagination, and just flirting with the others. She may have used one or another of them as a permissible substitute for some other unthinkable original.

3. She was in love with all of them and perhaps a dozen more over the years. Emily Dickinson was a vital human being and, even when she consciously protracted her girlhood, intensely a woman. She had a clear, hard, Edward Dickinson mind, but, like any poet, she knew that emotions are stronger than the mind, and hers were powerful.

4. The last possibility is just as tenable as any of the others. Emily Dickinson was in love with none of the men whose names have been mentioned in connection with hers. She may have been hopelessly and helplessly in love with someone whom conjecture has not reached and invention may never concoct. Emily Dickinson could keep a

secret—even, perhaps, the one that she had no actual lover but imagined one so ineffably wonderful that he could never have existed in the flesh.

Austin Dickinson said that his sister was attracted to a number of different men at various times in her life. Such feelings would be normal and natural, but they are not melodramatic enough. Brought up on Tennyson's Launcelot and Guinevere and his Lady of Shallot, doting on the love story of Robert and Elizabeth Barrett Browning—as Emily Dickinson doted on it—the Victorian world demanded that she have a love affair as star-crossed as that of Romeo and Juliet.

The more cynical twentieth-century world has likewise demanded annihilating romance to account for the life and writings of Emily Dickinson. The broken hearts of hundreds of thousands of shopgirls in penny-paper romances, the sentimental yearnings of the novel-reading and movie-going public, then the soap operas of radio and television have made many unwilling or unable to accept any other explanation.

In the end Mrs. Todd concluded that Emily Dickinson loved poetry better than she loved any man. This conclusion is sensible, honest, and may be right, or partly right, or nearly right. With Emily Dickinson, elusive, secretive, often perverse, it is impossible to be sure.

9

It would be nice, though a little dull, if life were arranged in a series of neat little blocks of incident, thought, and emotion, each self-contained and distinct. It is not. Events come pell-mell or dribble along, and our responses to them provoke a confusion of thoughts and feelings.

We live many lives at the same time: day-to-day physical lives of eating, sleeping, working, playing; religious and emotional lives; workaday lives; intellectual lives; and lives of daydreams and dreams asleep. We live, so to speak, on intersecting planes of consciousness and, for all we know, of unconsciousness too. If this is true for most people, it has to be markedly true of Emily Elizabeth Dickinson with her racing mind, her compelling emotions, and the myriad of contradictions in her character.

She was twenty-eight years old in December of 1858; Lavinia was twenty-six. Emily Fowler, Abby Wood, Helen Fiske, and most of their other school friends were married. The Dickinson girls were neither married nor engaged. They were already beyond the customary age for marriage, as undoubtedly village talk and attitudes made them well aware, and they were no longer girls. They were young women. Another generation of girls in their late teens and early twenties had taken their place as "young people" in Amherst.

Emily and Vinnie Dickinson lived on what was really a Yankee-feudal estate with household servants as well as hired men to see to the cleaning, the grounds, the gardens, and the horses, cows, pigs, and chickens in the big barn. The mansion was a big house requiring constant care. Emily Dickinson did all of the baking of bread and made most of the cakes, pies, and cookies. Though she disliked it, she did her share of the housework, even to lighting the wood fires in the early hours of cold winter mornings. She lived a full, demanding, and time-consuming practical life.

As she often complained in her letters, she had too little time to read and write. The time she valued more and more, as inner pressure—compelling necessity—to write developed in her, became harder to obtain and even more precious. Church took most of Sunday. The other house, "a hedge away," stole more of her time, but there the situation was changing.

Almost from the start Austin Dickinson was disappointed in his marriage. It was quickly apparent that he and his wife had different ideas and ideals. This was Susan Gilbert Dickinson's chance to parade her new possessions, her charm, and her lofty position as the wife of the "young Squire." She was determined to erase from people's minds, perhaps from her own, memories of her origin and upbringing and to substitute for them a picture of her as a brilliant and witty young hostess. She courted admiration and won it. If heightened emphasis and a few imagined details sometimes distorted the literal truth in what she said, she did not hesitate to use them for effect. Susan Dickinson was acute and articulate and careless of whom she might hurt.

One of Emily Dickinson's poems, "She dealt her pretty words like blades," thought to have been written about 1862, is supposedly about this penchant of her sister-in-law.

The relations between Susan Dickinson and her in-laws

grew more formal and polite, but, on the surface at any rate, the friendship of Sue and Emily remained strong. Like most friendships, it had its ups and downs. Emily Dickinson said she had one sister in the house and one a hedge away, but she also called Sue her "pseudo-sister." She sent Sue effusive notes, sometimes several times a day, and many of her poems, more than three hundred of them in all. Whatever differences they may have had, Susan Dickinson served her husband's sister well.

A musician cannot be sure he has been heard unless there is someone to listen and to applaud the sounds he makes. It is the same with any artist. A painter's work must be seen before he is assured he has painted well or badly. A poet must have a reader in order to be certain that he or she has created something that can be understood and appreciated. Otherwise the poem may be only something dreamed, even a distortion. Susan Dickinson served as audience to an artist who needed one and as a medium through which others heard the lines that Emily Dickinson wrote. She was not constrained to silence, so she read or showed them to guests. In her own way, Sue was necessary to Emily Dickinson.

Because of the growing disaffection between him and his wife, Austin was more frequently in his father's house. Emily and Lavinia sometimes found it hard to remember that he was married and actually lived elsewhere. Family solidarity hardened again, and so did its chief characteristic. Its members respected each other's idiosyncrasies. When Emily was not busy in the kitchen or her garden—outdoors in summer and in a conservatory off the dining room in winter—she spent more and more of her time by herself, but no one questioned it. That was her business. It was not their place to interfere or comment when she spent hours alone in her room. They assumed that she was reading or writing letters, for she kept up a large correspondence.

Emily Dickinson, of course, was spending much of this jealously hoarded time on her poetry. Sometimes she could dash off a poem, finding the exact phrase to fit the fleeting thought she had captured during the day. More often she wrote and rewrote, jotting down alternative choices to the nouns, verbs, and adjectives until she finally selected the best. She worked at white heat and with intense concentration.

When she was baking, she had her breadboard and flour near a window from which she could look out on the lawn and see a robin, a child, a passing stranger, a blue-jay, rain, a sunset, or a funeral going by. Anything might give her an idea. She kept pencil and paper handy to jot it down with flour-dusted fingers. Sometimes she wrote complete poems on the backs of recipes.

Something more important than even a tragic love affair had happened to Emily Dickinson. She had made a decision or helplessly acceded to an irresistible compulsion. She was in love with words and the patterns that she could make with them. This fact was major. Everything else was minor.

Meeting people in whom she had no particular interest, going to church or shopping in the village, making calls (usually with Carlo) and leaving the glazed card reading "Miss Emily E. Dickinson" no longer mattered to her. What really happened to Emily between 1857 and somewhere around 1860 was that she became Emily Dickinson. It was neither an abrupt change nor a reversal of what she had been all along.

Until she was twenty-five, twenty-six, or twenty-seven

years old, Emily Dickinson was just another witty and well-informed young woman. There were others in Amherst, and there were many brilliant, intelligent, and intellectual women in New England. She became distinctive when impulse became compulsion. This is a process of growth—if there is something to grow. Emily Dickinson was hardening into being as an artist.

The artist can be ruthless, sometimes has to be. His concern is self-realization and self-expression. Emily Dickinson became the most important person in the world to herself. It could not be otherwise. She stripped herself of what was superfluous to her thoughts and feelings and translated them into words. She stripped her manner of expression too. Her early letters and first attempts at verse had been discursive. She cut out all but essentials and forged a stabbing terseness for her lines.

She avoided people, even eventually people she loved, not because they interfered with the mere writing down of her poetry, but because they could disturb the delicate balance of idea, emotion, and expression which, though too intently to be conscious of it, she was trying to achieve. Poets, like other artists, seek seclusion for this reason. They are in themselves their ultimate resource and their ultimate being. While they are creating, no other reality exists.

When Emily Dickinson stripped her life and her verse of nonessentials she performed not two separate acts, but one. To her, poetry had become life, and she concentrated with blind ardor on living what was life to her. This was the turning point in her life both as an individual and as a poet.

Actually, there was no specific point, and no turning. What happened, happened inevitably on no particular day and was not caused by any incident or any person. It was not a turning. Instead, given her nature and talent, it was a straight line, as straight as she could make it, and she could make it very straight.

> The soul selects her own society,
> Then shuts the door;
> On her divine majority
> Obtrude no more.
>
> Unmoved, she notes the chariot's pausing
> At her low gate;
> Unmoved, an emperor is kneeling
> Upon her mat.
>
> I've known her from an ample nation
> Choose one;
> Then close the valves of her attention
> Like stone.

Note that the soul is "her," not "its." The poem, which Emily Dickinson wrote about 1862, is obviously autobiographical. She could explain her gradual withdrawal from those about her in a poem, but she did not attempt to explain it in life. She sent the first stanza of the poem to Susan Dickinson. Had Sue tried to see her and been refused? It is quite possible. Others had the same experience.

The year before that, Emily Dickinson had asked Sue's advice about one of her poems, sending it across the lawn for criticism. Sue did not really like it. Emily tried again, saying in a note that Sue might like the new version better. Sue still did not like the second stanza, so Emily attempted a new one. It did not satisfy her, so she returned to the original phrasing and sent the completed poem back with a note thanking Susan Dickinson for her criticism, saying she valued it. It was now she breathed the hope that some day her brother and sister-in-law would be proud of her. She did not again seek Sue's criticism.

The poem appeared unsigned but dated from the Pelham Hills, a place Emily Dickinson loved, in the *Springfield Republican,* March 1, 1862, in this form:

The Sleeping

Safe in their alabaster chambers
Untouched by morning,
  And untouched by noon,
Sleep the meek members of the Resurrection,
  Rafters of satin and roof of stone.

Light laughs the breeze
In her castle above them,
  Babbles the bee in a stolid ear,
Pipe the sweet birds in ignorant cadences;
  Ah! what sagacity perished here!

Death and the grave, nature—the subject was typically Dickinson, but the treatment in this early poem is conventional. Emily Dickinson no longer asked criticism of Sue or of any of the others near her. She knew it was useless, and she also knew exactly what poetry is. In a letter a few years later she wrote this:

> If I read a book, and it makes my whole body so cold no fire can ever warm me I know that it is poetry. If I feel physically as if the top of my head were taken off, I know that it is poetry. Is there any other way?

There is, of course, no other way. Critics may set up standards for the forms of poetry, decide what subjects are and are not suitable for poetic treatment, and lay down laws about language and style. They have done it since Aristotle, but they seldom satisfy anyone but themselves and perhaps some other critics.

Poets do not often go by rules. They say what they have to say in the only way they can say it. Those who hear or read their lines do not judge by rules but by whether the verse makes them feel more deeply the emotions the verse produces.

Emily Dickinson was soon writing poems that took the tops off heads.

By 1858 she had written enough poetry that she considered worth saving to begin copying the poems out in final form on notepaper and tying the sheets together with string in what at various times have been called volumes, fascicles, or packets. Sometimes she enclosed her worksheets or drafts of the poems showing alternative choices of words or phrases, as if she could not make up her mind which she liked best.

Because she made a fair copy of a poem in ink in 1858 or some other year does not necessarily mean she wrote it then. She did not date her poems. She gave titles to very few. Even the dates of letters in which she enclosed poems to friends are seldom proof of their date of origin because she often went back to her packets and selected one, sometimes changing it to fit the recipient or the occasion. The dates given for Emily Dickinson's poems are those that in recent years have been assigned on the basis of her handwriting. As does most people's, Emily Dickinson's handwriting changed over the years. It went from a flowing script to a peculiar mixture of script and lettering. Her method of punctuation changed too. She abandoned the ordinary punctuation used in her early letters to profuse use of the dash. These dashes, used both to connect and separate thoughts, gave speed to her lines. They carry the eye rapidly forward. Sometimes they seem gasps of joy or pain or indications of breathless excitement.

Cooking, doing housework, reading every book she could borrow or her father would buy for her, draining mind and heart for her poetry, Emily Dickinson had little time and no inclination for anything else. She did not leave the mansion and its grounds now even to go to Sue's. She lived her inner life at an emotional pitch and with a craftsman's concentration of which those around her could not even dream.

Ralph Waldo Emerson had lectured in the First Church in Amherst in 1857. Undoubtedly, Emily Dickinson had gone with all the others to hear him. Benjamin Franklin Newton had introduced her early to Emerson's poetry. She may even have met Emerson at Austin's house. Emerson's repeated advice was "Trust thyself"—trust your own instincts, insist on yourself, never imitate, build your own world. Emily Dickinson never tried to be anyone else, she did not imitate, and she was building her own world.

Henry David Thoreau was Emerson's young friend and disciple in Concord. Undoubtedly again, Emily Dickinson knew his *A Week on the Concord and Merrimack Rivers,* which was published in 1849, and read *Walden* after its appearance in 1854.

She was a lady of parlors and sitting rooms, conservatories and polished furniture. Graceful and gracious, she might have found rough-edged and rustic Henry Thoreau too graceless for the Dickinson mansion. She had no wish to live by herself in the woods, as Thoreau had done, but she would have known what he meant when he talked. Is the value of a man in his skin that I should touch

(87)

him? Thoreau demanded. Emily Dickinson did not think it was. Live life near the bone where it is sweetest, Thoreau advised. Emily Dickinson lived there. Advance confidently in the direction of your dreams and you will meet with a success unexpected in common hours. Emily Dickinson advanced confidently. She did something else on which Thoreau insisted. She wrote while the white heat was in her.

Thoreau was no more lonely than the loon in Walden Pond. Neither was Emily Dickinson. She found the mere living of every day almost more exciting than she could bear. She withdrew more and more into her solitude and out of it came poems startling in their insight and originality. Some of them were about nature, but Emily Dickinson was not really a nature poet. She wrote of flowers, birds about the house, gardens, even a garden snake, much as a housewife might. Her real and almost her sole subject was herself, her thoughts, her emotions, but sometimes she wrote from what seems sheer exuberance.

> If recollecting were forgetting,
>   Then I remember not;
> And if forgetting, recollecting,
>   How near I had forgot!
> And if to miss were merry,
>   And if to mourn were gay,
> How very blithe the fingers
>   That gathered these to-day.

She sent the poem to Samuel Bowles with a note signed "Emilie." There is gaiety in the verse, play on thought and words, fondness. She wrote more serious poetry in this same year of 1859.

I never lost as much but twice,
And that was in the sod;
Twice have I stood a beggar
Before the door of God!

Angels twice descending
Reimbursed my store.
Burglar, banker, father,
I am poor once more!

Death again, but how different this is from "Safe in their alabaster chambers." The sharpness, almost the starkness, of the first stanza, paints a vivid picture in cold black and white. Flippancy does not disguise the feeling in the second stanza. Few people address God as burglar, banker, and father, but Emily Dickinson could. The poem is said to refer to the deaths of Humphrey and Newton.

Poets, as Emerson pointed out, cannot write poetry by an act of will. They cannot write it on demand. Poets will save for years something they once wrote but present as new. Emily Dickinson wrote this next poem about 1859 and sent a copy to Susan Dickinson. It became the one poem published in a book during her lifetime. After much coaxing she allowed it to appear anonymously in *A Masque of Poets* in the late fall of 1878.

Success is counted sweetest
By those who ne'er succeed.
To comprehend a nectar
Requires sorest need.

Not one of all the purple host
Who took the flag to-day
Can tell the definition,
So clear, of victory

(89)

As he, defeated, dying,
On whose forbidden ear
The distant strains of triumph
Break, agonized and clear.

There were Dickinson nature poems in the late 1850's, but one was so outspoken that her first editors hesitated about printing it. Fortunately they decided to risk the sexual imagery, which seemed to them to verge on eroticism.

Did the harebell loose her girdle
To the lover bee,
Would the bee the harebell hallow
Much as formerly?

Did the paradise, persuaded,
Yield her moat of pearl,
Would the Eden be an Eden,
Or the earl an earl?

The poems were becoming stronger in tone, bolder in statement. Some were charged with joy or pain that seems almost out of control. These are the exquisitely personal and unabashed Dickinson poems that take the tops off heads. They seem almost to have removed Emily Dickinson's at times.

The pressures were mounting, and she had so constrained her existence that there were no distractions to ease. She was torn by conflicting desires. She wanted publication and fame. "Success" did not come out of thin air but out of her own experience. She wanted fulfillment in ways of which she dreamed. She wanted—she did not know quite what. Probably everything.

At once bold and shy, she was at the same time weak and strong. She was outspoken and enigmatic. She was clear and esoteric. She was direct as few men are direct and more indirect than most women. Then one day she wrote a letter to a perfect stranger asking the advice and help she seemed alternately to beg and rebuff from those, like Samuel Bowles and Josiah Holland, who were close to her.

In the introduction to still another edition of Emily Dickinson's letters, this one published in 1951 and again in 1962, Mark Van Doren says that this letter and the correspondence which ensued may have been the climax of her life. Wisely he adds, "Yet one cannot say for sure. Her life was all climax. . . ."

10

Born December 22, 1823, in Cambridge, where his father was bursar of Harvard, Thomas Wentworth Higginson was early attracted to books and became an omnivorous reader. Naturally he went to Harvard. After graduation he taught for two years, then returned to Harvard for three years of leisurely graduate study. In 1846 he entered the senior class of the Harvard Divinity School, took his degree, and became a Unitarian minister of the most liberal kind. Thus, Higginson was academic without being professorial and a minister without being ministerial.

For a few years he preached in Newburyport and Worcester, but his inclinations lay elsewhere. He was a militant Abolitionist who did not shrink from violent action. In Boston he helped rescue runaway slaves who were about to be returned to their owners under the Fugitive Slave Act. Twice he went west to fight against slavery in Kansas.

Higginson was also an active proponent of woman suffrage and an outspoken feminist. As a minister in Worcester he presided at the marriage of Lucy Stone, a leader of the women's rights movement of the time. By continuing to use her maiden name after marriage she founded the Lucy Stone League of women who followed her example.

Tall, rather awkward, an athlete, Higginson was a reformer. He was also literary to the tips of his long, tapering fingers. He was a poet and an essayist, and well known as a lecturer. In April 1862 he contributed the lead article to the *Atlantic Monthly*. In "Letter to a Young Contributor" he told young writers to work hard, avoid pretentious language, work for a smooth style, and, above all, to put life into their writing.

Emily Dickinson read the piece. Like most magazine articles of the time, it was unsigned, but she learned from the *Springfield Republican* who had written it. April 16, 1862, she wrote Higginson this letter:

> Mr. Higginson.—Are you too deeply occupied to say if my verse is alive?
>
> The mind is so near itself it cannot see distinctly, and I have none to ask.
>
> Should you think it breathed, and had you the leisure to tell me, I should feel quick gratitude.
>
> If I make the mistake, that you dared to tell me would give me sincere honor toward you.
>
> I inclose my name, asking you, if you please, sir, to tell me what is true?
>
> That you will not betray me it is needless to ask, since honor is its own pawn.

She did not sign the letter but enclosed, hidden in its own smaller envelope, a card on which she had written her name in pencil.

This is the way Emily Dickinson had begun to talk in her letters as in some of her verse, perhaps even to herself. The abrupt one-sentence paragraphs, the odd expressions, the teasing indirectness. She had become—a favorite word of hers—oblique. As Higginson was to say several times, she was "enigmatical."

Translated, her letter said: "I read your article. I am a young writer. Here are some of my poems. Will you be good enough to tell me whether they are good or bad, i.e., publishable. I am too close to my own work to know. If you cannot do this, I will understand, but I will be grateful if you can. Please don't tell anyone."

Such letters are written by the thousands to established authors, who usually do not know what to do with them or how to answer. Obviously this letter was different from most. Higginson recognized this immediately. The Civil War was on. No mere litterateur but a man of action who saw the war as an onslaught on slavery, Higginson had been made captain of a volunteer company he had raised and was about to leave for military duty. Despite this, he answered Emily Dickinson immediately.

She had enclosed four poems: "Safe in their alabaster chambers"; "Success is counted sweetest"; "I'll tell you how the sun rose"; and "We play at paste till qualified for pearl." Higginson was struck with their originality and said so, but Emily Dickinson had asked for advice along the lines of his article. He noticed the lack of punctuation in the poems, the haphazard capitalization, the occasional lapses in grammar, and pointed them out.

Only ten days after her first letter, and apologizing even then for delay caused by illness, which could not have been serious, Emily Dickinson wrote Higginson again. She thanked him for his "surgery," enclosed more of her verses, and—in her own way—answered some of the questions he had asked.

"You asked how old I was? I made no verses, but one or two, until this winter, sir."

Not only did Emily Dickinson avoid telling her age, which was thirty-one, but she deliberately misled the stranger whose help she had sought. She had written scores of poems and, even as she wrote Higginson, was writing tempestuous verse, which she did not show him.

There is some indication of it in the very next paragraph of this well-known letter.

The paragraph bore no relation to what had gone before. It seems to have been blurted out as an impulsive aside, but Emily Dickinson usually knew what she was about only too well. She needed the relief of explanation and confession. "I had a terror since September, I could tell to none; and so I sing as the boy does by the burying ground because I am afraid."

Those who favor the theory believe that she referred to Wadsworth's leaving Philadelphia for San Francisco. Others find varied explanations. None fit. Emily Dickinson simply wanted to tell someone something, yet, as so often, she could not bring herself to be explicit.

"I have a brother and sister, my mother does not care for thought, and father, too busy with his briefs to notice what we do. He buys me many books, but begs me not to read them, because he fears they joggle the mind. They are religious except me, and address an eclipse, every morning, whom they call their 'Father.' "

This damning description of her family is not to be taken literally. Mrs. Dickinson was no intellectual, but that does not mean she was unintelligent. Practical Edward Dickinson would not have purchased books to go unread. He was not too busy with his briefs to care deeply for his family and their good. Emily Dickinson's graphic description in her typical shorthand is clever, but fair neither to them nor to herself.

The others had been converted and went to church, which she no longer did. Thus they were religious and she who stayed home and avoided family prayers was not. Emily Dickinson was deeply religious, continually aware of God and the immortality she wrote so much about. It was the manner, not the matter, of religion she spoke of to Higginson.

She bitterly wished for fame, which could not come without publication of her poetry. Undoubtedly she hoped at this time that Higginson could help get her work published, but she wrote, "Two editors of journals came to my father's house this winter, and asked me for my mind, and when I asked them 'why' they said I was penurious, and they would use it for the world."

Clearly she meant Bowles and Holland, who had already printed some of her poems. They had not come just that winter but many times. Emily Dickinson could be coy. Her repeated insistence later that she did not wish her verse to be published has always smacked too much of "the lady doth protest too much." To the end of her life, though not always directly, she was always bringing her poems to the attention of those she thought might publish them. Instead of meaning to discourage Higginson she may well have meant to entice. Other editors were already seeking her work.

It has long been fashionable to blame T. W. Higginson for not seeing immediately that he dealt with genius and introducing Emily Elizabeth Dickinson to the world with a fanfare of trumpets. He had little to go on. She had not sent him any of the intensely personal verse that has since brought her acclaim. She gave him the impression that she was just beginning to write verse. He thought she was a young girl. He was pressed for time, for war was convulsing the nation. Instead of going as captain of the regiment he had raised, Higginson had accepted the colonelcy of the first Negro regiment of the North.

Emily Dickinson puzzled him. He felt he understood her a little better when by chance he met her father's brother. William Dickinson was a prominent businessman of Worcester. In him Higginson found the same impulsiveness and abruptness he found in the letters of his niece, though he says they did not share the poetic temperament—"from which he was indeed singularly remote."

Higginson did not even know what Emily Dickinson looked like. When he asked for a picture, she had none to send. She told him that she disliked having her picture taken. Her father (it is always her father, never her mother) had pictures of all the others and warned her that "death might occur," but he got none of her.

Nor do we know what Emily Dickinson looked like either. The only likenesses that exist are the childhood portrait of the three children, the silhouette of the schoolchild, and the Mount Holyoke daguerreotype which the family said did not look like her. Curls were plastered on a reproduction of it and a fluffy ruff placed around her neck for the falsified picture made familiar to the public when it appeared in one of the books about her in the 1920's.

Emily Ford said that Emily Dickinson had great beauties, just as Lavinia said her sister had had many advantageous offers of marriage but refused them all to stay with her. Women say these things out of courtesy or affection. Others who saw Emily Dickinson at various times during her life have described her as plain without a single good feature, as tiny, as wraithlike, as a typical New England spinster. MacGregor Jenkins, who knew her when he was a small boy and Emily Dickinson was in her forties, said she was a beautiful woman dressed in white with soft, fiery brown eyes and a mass of tawny hair. He says her voice was low, clear-toned, and sweet.

It was in explaining why she had no picture to send that Emily Dickinson painted her delightfully worded self-portrait for Higginson. It was written as carefully as any of her poems. ". . . small, like the wren, and my hair is bold like the chestnut burr; and my eyes like the sherry in the glass the guest leaves."

The wren is a neat and shapely bird. Comparison with it conveys the idea of grace in form and flight. The chestnut is a shining brownish red. Reference to both bird and burr tells of Emily Dickinson's closeness to nature. The sherry tells not only of a color but also that the Dickinsons lived in becoming style. There is honesty in Emily Dickinson's description of herself and also a touching vanity. Few saw her, and sometimes she must have wished to be seen. She could have told Higginson that she was short and redheaded.

Evidently, Higginson told her now that he thought it best for her to delay attempting publication of her poems. She accepted his judgment agreeably, for it was **pleasant** for her—it was, in fact, dire necessity—to have someone knowledgeable to whom she could talk seriously about her work. She sent him, June 6, 1862, a copy of her "Renunciation," but it is a mistake to assume that she accepted Higginson's judgment as final and from this point on renounced all hope of publication during her lifetime. It is a mistake to read much of Emily Dickinson, poems or letters, literally. Her imagination lights her lines. So does her humor, her mockery, her obliqueness. She had her private jokes in her inscrutable notes and sometimes in her verse. Emily Dickinson wrote to please herself, and the teasing indirectness is as much a part of her as her blinding insight and her pleasure in pithy aphorisms.

She wrote Higginson in an evasive generality, "If fame belonged to me, I could not escape her; if she did not, the longest day would pass me on the chase, and the approbation of my dog would forsake me then." That is not renunciation but detached observation, not too original. The mention of the dog her father had bought her is pure Dickinson. She valued Carlo's approval.

Despite their humor and the seriousness thinly disguised by flippancy, there is a pleading note in these early letters to Higginson. Repeatedly she asked him to be her "preceptor." She signed her letters "Your friend, E. Dickinson," just "Your friend," more often, "Your scholar," and once, in 1863, when Colonel Higginson was in camp in South Carolina, "Your gnome."

This signature mystified the colonel. What did she mean? Was there some reference he had missed? He could not explain it. Neither, probably, could Emily Dickinson. Perhaps she just felt like a gnome that day. It is possible to feel like a wren one day, an ox the next, a gnome or what have you the day following.

She was sure and then she was unsure about her poetry. She needed Higginson's reassurance, and she got it from a generous and perceptive man and writer. Perhaps he was not a prophet, but there are seldom many around. He could not know what Emily Dickinson did not tell him, or understand the partial revelations, which gave her the release she sought without saying too much. One day she had been sure, though, for when she sent Higginson her first tentative letter, she also included this poem:

> We play at paste
> Till qualified for pearl,
> Then drop the paste,
> And deem ourself a fool.

The shapes, though, were similar,
And our new hands
Learned gem-tactics
Practicing sands.

Emily Dickinson knew when she wrote this poem that she had learned her trade. She was no longer an apprentice but a journeyman. For some years, she told Higginson, after the death of her "dying tutor" her lexicon had been her only companion. She had studied it well. She loved words. They were the gems, and hers were the tactics. She had played at paste in her early valentines. The opening lines of the one sent Elbridge Bowdoin in 1850 were:

Awake ye muses nine, sing me a strain divine,
Unwind the solemn twine, and tie my Valentine!
Oh, the Earth was *made* for lovers, for damsel and hopeless
swain
For sighing and gentle whispering, and *unity* made of *twain*.
All things do go a courting, in earth, or sea, or air.
God hath made nothing single but thee in His world
so fair! . . .

In this nonsense verse the invocation to the Muses, the poetic diction, the grammar and punctuation are all as correct as any of Emily Dickinson's Amherst Academy teachers could have wished. Her rhymes are exact—and the whole is paste.

The fourteen-stanza valentine to William Howland in 1852 was just as correct.

Hurrah for Peter Parley!
Hurrah for Daniel Boon!

Three cheers, sir, for the gentleman
Who first observed the moon!

Peter, put up the sunshine;
Pattie, arrange the stars,
Tell Luna, *tea* is waiting,
And call your brother Mars!

Put down the apple, Adam,
And come away with me,
So shalt thou have a *pippin*
From off my father's tree

The paste is gay nonsense and punning cleverness, but there is one stanza that sounds like the later Dickinson in its humor, irony, and use of huge, abstract words.

Mortality is fatal—
Gentility is fine,
Rascality, heroic,
Insolvency, sublime!

Emily Dickinson was already working her way to pearls, and there is a strong connection between these early comic valentines and the most poignant poems of her poetic maturity.

The valentines were about love. Love was the chief subject of conversation among "the girls." It led to engagements and marriage. Those who achieved the desired end could then go about their business of being secure in the conjugal state and forget all about love. Emily Dickinson, who did not achieve the shared objective, could not forget.

Her love poetry is a natural sequence to the valentines. Her poems of love are the more intense because her love was not realized. Emily Dickinson knew this.

Who never wanted—maddest joy
Remains to him unknown.
The banquet of abstemiousness
Surpasses that of wine.

Emily Dickinson did not write this poem until about
1877, but she had lived its truth for many years.

She did not send Higginson any of her intensely personal love poetry. Attributed mostly to 1860 and 1861,
the years immediately before she approached him, are the
poems of diamond sharpness, dazzling clarity, and searing
passion that almost must have burned the paper she wrote
them on.

I'm wife, I've finished that,
That other state;
I'm Czar, I'm woman now;
It's safer so.

How odd the girl's life looks
Behind this soft eclipse!
I think the earth seems so
To those in heaven now.

In 1861 came "Heaven is what I cannot reach," "What
would I give to see his face," "Doubt me, my dim companion," and "Read, sweet, how others strove." There
was also this most abandoned and triumphant of all her
love poems:

Wild nights! Wild nights!
Were I with thee,
Wild nights should be
Our luxury.

Futile the winds
To a heart in port,—
Done with the compass,
Done with the chart.

Rowing in Eden!
Ah! The sea!
Might I but moor
To-night in thee!

There was ecstasy in that. There is pain in this:

Doubt me, my dim companion!
Why, God would be content
With but a fraction of the love
Poured thee without a stint.
The whole of me, forever,
What more the woman can,—
Say quick, that I may dower thee
With last delight I own.

No one could live at this pitch of emotion and retain his sanity. Emily Dickinson could not. At the same time she was writing less passionate but equally vibrant poetry which spoke the sheer delight in living that in itself made life almost too much for her.

I taste a liquor never brewed,
From tankards scooped in pearl,
Not all the vats upon the Rhine
Yield such an alcohol.

Inebriate of air am I,
And debauchee of dew,
Reeling through endless summer days
From inns of molten blue.

When landlords turn the drunken bee
Out of the foxglove's door,
When butterflies renounce their drams,
I shall but drink the more!

Till seraphs swing their snowy hats,
And saints to windows run,
To see the little tippler
Leaning against the sun!

Sheer gladness sings through the happy lines of that poem, which was published in the *Springfield Republican*, May 4, 1861, but Emily Dickinson at the same time felt and understood its opposite.

I like a look of agony,
Because I know it's true.
Men do not sham convulsion
Nor simulate a throe. . . .

Emily Dickinson knew exactly what she was writing, and it is easily described. It is poetry that made her whole body so cold no fire could ever warm her and made her feel physically as if the top of her head had been taken off.

Small wonder she remained within her father's house and grounds and, as much as she could, in her upstairs room with its windows overlooking East Main Street in one direction, Austin's house in another. The joy and wonder she reached in creation there could not be matched elsewhere. Thomas Wentworth Higginson? She had to discover herself to someone to retain her sanity.

She was the ultimate Dickinson, possessed of all the reserve, secretiveness, and self-sufficiency that made the Edward Dickinsons different. She was also—word invented to describe the indescribable—a genius.

11

Squire Dickinson must have realized that he had two oddities for daughters. Emily was a recluse. Vinnie, away for weeks at a time to visit relatives, was belligerent and virulent. At any rate, the two young women lived at home, where he could look after them, and Edward Dickinson *was* busy with his briefs. He handled divorce cases, settled estates, pled minor criminal as well as civil cases, and gave much of his energy and acumen to Amherst College, both managing its finances and planning and overseeing the construction of new buildings.

The railroad station was only a few hundred yards down the hill of East Main Street, on six acres of what had once been Dickinson land. Often Edward Dickinson took an early train for Boston or even more distant places for political conventions or whatever his business or public interests called for. When he was away, he wrote his family almost daily. His concern for their welfare never slackened.

Austin was not only his father's associate; he was becoming virtually his replica. He lacked his father's sternness and liking for politics. He had more imagination, but he was as clearheaded and as definite. Austin had the disappointment of his marriage to endure as best he could. The mansion was his refuge. He went there daily, and on mornings when business took him out of town he stopped on his way to the train. He left town as seldom as he could. More and more his interests centered in Amherst.

His older sister's growing detachment from the world did not perturb Austin. Her eccentricity, if it was that, was just the Dickinson eccentricity in slightly more acute form. Years later he would say that he thought it was because Emily was aware of her plainness that she kept so much out of sight.

Everyone did not accept her withdrawal with the same equanimity. Long a favorite with her, as with the rest of the Dickinsons, Samuel Bowles did not. On one occasion when he came to the house and Emily fled, he would have none of it. From the downstairs hall he shouted up to her, "Emily, you damned rascal, no more of this nonsense! I've traveled all the way from Springfield to see you. Come down at once!"

To the amazement of the others, Emily obediently came, and Vinnie says she had never been more brilliant in conversation. A few days later Emily Dickinson sent Bowles one of her frequent humorous notes. She signed this one "Your Rascal" and added gaily, "I washed the adjective."

Her sense of humor was always there. She had begun writing as the wit of *Forest Leaves*. Her early letters were full of fun. Prose or verse, her valentines were comic. Dry, sly, sometimes ironic, humor sparkles in her letters and lurks in many of her most serious poems.

This was the balancing ingredient in her character and in her writings. No one could live without relief in the rarefied atmosphere she had deliberately created for herself. At the same time that she was writing her most trenchant poetry, she was quipping and jesting in her letters and writing of simple everyday things. She wrote Fanny and Louise Norcross about her sewing, cooking, the weather, Carlo, their stalwart maid Maggie, and of their shopping for a hood. She wrote oftenest, perhaps, of her flowers. These letters, effusive in their expressions of love and affection, she signed "Emily" or "Emilie" as it pleased her, sometimes just "Sister" and once "Poor Plover." Sometimes she addressed them as "Dear Children," and often she referred to herself in the third person as "Emily." That was one of her habits, and was part of her teasing endearments, the childlikeness she liked to assume, and her way of standing a little way off and looking back at herself.

Like any ordinary mortal, Emily Dickinson was much a part of what went on around her, even to spring house-cleaning—she said she preferred pestilence. She read the *Republican, Scribner's, Harper's,* the *Atlantic,* and other magazines. She listened to the Amherst church bells and the Amherst gossip. Home and her own village were as dear to her as they had been when she was a homesick Mount Holyoke student. Henry Thoreau had described himself as a great traveler around Concord. Emily Dickinson was "a great traveler around Amherst," even though she did not cross her father's threshold and grounds to go to any other town or any other house. She used this phrase to Higginson when he asked her to see him when she came to Boston, "as all ladies do."

Emily Dickinson seems to have been largely unaware of the Civil War. Perhaps she tried to keep it from her consciousness. Once she mentions a soldier who came to the mansion one day and asked for a nosegay to take with him to the war. She spoke of him as of someone strange, as she might have spoken of a tramp or a beggar. She also grieved for an Amherst widow who lost both her sons in battle, and at one point the war did come sharply home to her.

Son of President William Augustus Stearns of Amherst College, Frazer Stearns was one of the first of hundreds of Amherst students to volunteer. With everyone else in Amherst who knew him, Emily Dickinson prayed he would be safe. He was killed in the battle of New Bern, North Carolina. Always fascinated by death, Emily Dickinson wrote of it feelingly to her Norcross cousins.

. . . He fell by the side of Professor Clark, his superior officer—lived ten minutes in a soldier's arms, asked twice for water—murmured just, "My God," and passed! Sanderson, his classmate, made a box of boards in the night, and put the brave boy in, covered with a blanket, rowed six miles to reach the boat,—so poor Frazer came. They tell me that Colonel Clark cried like a little child when he missed his pet, and could hardly resume his post. They loved each other very much. Nobody could look on Frazer—not even his father. The doctors would not allow it.

The bed on which he came was enclosed in a large casket shut entirely, and covered from head to foot with the sweetest flowers. He went to sleep from the village church. Crowds came to tell him good-night, choirs sang to him, pastors told how brave he was—early-soldier heart. And the family bowed their heads, as the reeds the wind shakes.

. . . Austin is completely stunned. . . .

Austin himself, then just thirty-five, was drafted into the Union Army in May 1864. He did not go. As was permitted practice at the time, he paid five hundred dollars for a substitute to go in his place.

Colonel Thomas Wentworth Higginson was wounded that same month and invalided out of the army.

Emily Dickinson must have written letters almost daily. She wrote long letters, cryptic letters, arch letters. She wrote notes to accompany gifts of cake, flowers, or wine. Often she enclosed poems. Sometimes the poem itself was the message. However, in the early 1860's she wrote at least three letters of a very different kind. They are heart-tearing letters of ecstasy and utter despair, which provoke awe, compassion, and almost physical pain. They must have left Emily Dickinson numb with exhaustion. Perhaps that is one reason she wrote them. The letters, in which she refers to herself as "Daisy," were addressed to someone she called "Master."

A small part of one of them was included in *Letters of Emily Dickinson,* published by Mabel Loomis Todd in 1894. The opening sentence is both startling and moving.

> If you saw a bullet hit a bird, and he told you he wasn't shot, you might weep at his courtesy, but you would certainly doubt his word.

Emily Dickinson had been hurt and could not pretend otherwise. She had found her heart too big to hold, offered it, and, evidently, had the offer refused. There is anguish in the way she tells of it, pain in the way she asks her "Master" if he will not come to New England. She promises not to disappoint, says that even to see his face would be unutterable joy.

She says nothing that clearly, of course. Her letter is cryptic. It is as if, as so often, she wishes at once to disclose and stay hidden. Her language is metaphorical and even here touched with her mockery. "Thomas's faith in anatomy was stronger than his faith in faith . . . Vesuvius don't talk—Aetna don't. One of them said a syllable a thousand years ago, and Pompeii heard it and hid forever.

She couldn't look the world in the face afterward, I suppose. Bashful Pompeii. . . ."

The full texts of the "Master" letters were not made public until 1955, when they were published by Millicent Todd Bingham.

The letters were found in corrected drafts among Emily Dickinson's papers. They bore no date. There is no indication who "Master" was. Possibly, as Mrs. Bingham pointed out, they were meant for Wadsworth but more likely for Bowles. Both men were out of New England at the time. It is just as possible that they were meant for someone else or for no one, some man envisioned and made the object of an almost frightening love. Whether fair copies of these drafts were ever sent is unknown. They bear careful corrections and notes for substitute phrases, just as if they were poetry intended for publication.

The woman who wrote these letters to a real or imagined "master" was not at peace. Her pleading is anguished; her rapture wild. They are the pain with an "element of blank" of which she wrote in one of her astringent poems. Emily Dickinson could scarcely survive the onslaught of what she had called forth.

In late 1863 her eyes gave out. She had been reading and writing, often late at night by lamp or candlelight, for a long time. Her eyes must have been badly strained. She read incessantly. Casual references in her letters show how familiar she was with both the English poetry of the past and the books that were popular when she wrote of them.

She was not a scholar or even a student of literature. She was a poet, not a critic. She read for pleasure, for stimulation, for ideas. She knew the Bible and Shakespeare thoroughly, of course, but she could get just as excited about Ik Marvel or the sentimental and religious novels of Elizabeth Stuart Phelps. The Brontë sisters and George Eliot were among her favorites.

> There is no frigate like a book
> To take us lands away,
> Nor any coursers like a page
> Of prancing poetry . . .

Emily Dickinson knew the English and American poets, essayists, and historians. Byron was another favorite. She read Hawthorne and said she was both enticed and appalled by his dark tales. She knew Thomson's "Seasons" and Young's "Night Thoughts." She read Emerson, Thoreau, and Lowell, but was just as enthusiastic about Harriet Beecher Stowe, Dr. Holland, later Helen Hunt Jackson, and, of course, everything that Thomas Wentworth Higginson wrote. She knew Dickens so well that she and Austin wrote letters identifying themselves with characters in his books.

Besides books that her father brought her she had books borrowed from the college library and ordered books that she saw advertised in her newspapers and magazines. She made and received gifts of books throughout her life. There are echoes of many other poets in her work: Shakespeare, Donne, Quarles, Keats, Byron. She even knew—and did not like—the popular Joaquin Miller. Emily Dickinson was not just well read. She was a book-saturated woman who added what books told her to what she had experienced or imagined and melted the whole into her work.

Reading and writing alone could have accounted for what she sometimes called her long illness and sometimes described as the time when her eyes were put out. She began to experience sharp eye discomfort before the end of 1863, when the difficulty was severe enough for Vinnie to take her to Boston to consult an occulist.

Her eyes had become hypersensitive to light. She could not bear the glare of the sun on the snow even when she was inside the house and protected from it. Strain induced by abuse of her eyes in poor light had to be part of the cause, but because the reaction of the eyes to the nerves and emotions as well as to physical ailments is well known, it has often been conjectured that Emily Dickinson's eye trouble was emotional and psychological in origin. Whatever the cause, Emily Dickinson was forced to leave home and Amherst for more than half of 1864 and again for seven months in 1865 to have her eyes treated in Boston.

When she had to, Emily Dickinson could face the world. She faced it during those years from a boarding-house in Cambridgeport, where she lived with Fanny and Louise Norcross. She did not like it. Though she was forbidden to, she wrote. She could read a little. The visits to the occulist were painful. Worst was the procession of strangers who came and went in the boardinghouse. She called the place a prison, but admitted that prisoners came to like their cages. Byron's prisoner of Chillon, she noted, had wanted to go back to his dungeon after he was freed from it. She missed her home badly and begged to know every detail of what was happening there. Her cousins were as kind as they could be, but was the lettuce up in the garden?

Higginson was in a hospital recovering from the effects of his wound in 1864 (he mistakenly says 1863, but Hawthorne did not die until mid-May 1864) when he received this letter.

Dear Friend,—Are you in danger? I did not know that you were hurt. Will you tell me more. Mr. Hawthorne died.

I was ill since September, and since April in Boston for a physician's care. He does not let me go, yet I work in my prison, and make guests for myself.

Carlo did not come, because that he would die in jail, and the mountains I could not hold now, so I brought but the Gods.

I wish to see you more than before I failed. Will you tell me your health? I am surprised and anxious since receiving your note.

> The only news I know
> Is bulletins all day
> From immortality.

Can you render my pencil? The physician has taken away my pen. I inclose the address from a letter, lest my figures fail. Knowledge of your recovery would excel my own.

E. Dickinson

Emily Dickinson worried about her flower garden. Cousin Lou wanted to send Austin a picture of the capture of Jefferson Davis but feared he would think her frivolous. Women, she wrote Vinnie, did not wear bonnets in Boston. Once she wrote, "the drums keep on for the still man—. . ." (Abraham Lincoln). She hoped the two teeth missing in the front yard of the mansion had been filled —with hemlock. She longed for home.

Release came finally. The occulist would see her for the last time on the Monday of Thanksgiving week 1865, and she would be set free from her Cambridgeport prison the next day. She instructed Vinnie to meet her train at Palmer, ordering her firmly to come by herself alone. "Let no one else come."

Emily Elizabeth Dickinson returned to Amherst and her father's house November 28, 1865. She never left them again.

12

After he left the army and recovered from his war injuries Thomas Wentworth Higginson lived with his invalid wife (a sister of Ellery Channing, Thoreau's poet walking companion) in a boardinghouse in Newport, Rhode Island.

He went to work on a novel, a history of his war experiences, a biography, and criticism. His reputation as a lecturer and as a magazine writer continued to mount, and his correspondence with Emily Dickinson continued unabated. She sent him copies of many of her poems. He many times planned to visit her, but circumstances and his commitments interfered until August 16, 1870. Then for the first time he met her in her father's home.

Fortunately he made notes of their meeting and sent them that night in a letter to his wife. He used them when he wrote an article about Emily Dickinson for the *Atlantic* after her death.

He was admitted to the mansion.

After a little delay, I heard an extremely faint and pattering footstep like that of a child, in the hall, and in glided, almost noiselessly, a plain, shy little person, the face without a single good feature, but with eyes, as she herself said, "like the sherry the guest leaves in the glass," and with smooth bands of reddish chestnut hair. She had a quaint and nun-like look, as if she might be a German canoness of some religious order, whose prescribed garb was white pique, with a blue net worsted shawl. She came toward me with two day-lillies, which she put in a childlike way into my hand, saying softly, under her breath, "These are my introduction," and also adding, under her breath in child-like fashion, "Forgive me if I am frightened; I never see strangers, and hardly know what I say."

Emily Dickinson must have dreaded this meeting to which she had looked forward so long and so eagerly. She was thirty-nine years old. She went nowhere, not even to Austin's. She saw few visitors, avoiding even family intimates. She wore nothing but white.

Yet, once the first shock of unaccustomed adventure was over, she talked almost without interruption, as if she were starved. In her loneliness she had prepared and rehearsed what she had to say. She spoke quickly and in aphorisms. It was almost as if she had written down and corrected, then memorized her words. She spoke in the language of writing rather than in the more casual manner of ordinary conversation.

Regardless of her effect on him as listener, Higginson noted, she talked for her own relief. She told him of her early life, and, Higginson acutely observed, her father was always the chief figure in it. She kept on talking: "Is it oblivion or absorption when things pass from our minds?" —"Truth is such a rare thing that it is delightful to tell it."—"If I read a book and it makes my whole body so cold. . . ."—"Women talk. That is why I dread women."

Emily Dickinson was on parade. She wanted to impress this man of the literary world, yet, even in this unique meeting, her humor did not desert her. "How do most people live without any thoughts? There are many people in the world—you must have noticed them in the streets. . . . How do they get strength to put on their clothes in the morning?"

When Higginson asked her if she did not feel constricted in her seclusion and feel the need to move about and see other people, Emily Dickinson had her answer prepared. "I never thought of conceiving that I could ever have the slightest approach to such a want in all future time." Then she added, "I feel that I have not expressed myself strongly enough."

Higginson saw Emily again the next morning and met her father, whom he described as a real Puritan, dry and speechless. He found Emily herself natural and unaffected. He liked her, but admitted that he could not fully comprehend her. She seemed to cast a spell, he said, and the meeting with her left him drained of energy.

When they parted, he promised to come again some time. Instantly, Emily Dickinson rejoined, "Say, in a long time, that will be nearer. Some time is no time."

"Quaint and nun-like," Emily Dickinson appeared to Higginson. Perhaps it was the impression she wished to make, for she liked to dramatize herself. She was not quaint, and she was not nunlike in character or thought. What Higginson had really seen was a quiescent volcano, a deer captured in midleap, a rainbow muted for courtesy—take your choice.

There was a sentimental streak in Emily Dickinson. It shows in her nature verse, in the exaggerated endearments and gushing affection of many of her letters. There was a strong domestic streak. She could write Louise Norcross that she had cooked the peaches as she told her and they were delicious; and that the beans made a savory cream when fricasseed. She told Higginson that she baked all the family bread because her father would eat no other.

There was a rootless, restless streak in Emily Dickinson. "My business is circumference," she said. She wanted to know everything everywhere. Africa was as much her concern as Main Street. At the same time there was an unshakable love of her own place. Amherst was the center of the world, and she was not only in it and of it but felt that she *was* it. Sometimes she called herself "Amherst," even signed herself "Amherst."

There was a deep religious streak in Emily Dickinson. Inheritor of the Puritan tradition and influenced by the more liberal thought of Emerson, she accepted without question the established beliefs of her time. There was this life and the next, both certain. It was the details, not the basic creed, of evangelical Protestantism that she questioned.

Emily wanted desperately to be a complete woman, yet wished and tried to remain a child. She had a bedrock honesty with an ever-present vein of humor running through a mother lode of grim seriousness. She was intensely feminine. Her attitude toward love was feminine. Yet she had her father's clear and very masculine directness and his logic.

Emily Dickinson could write from the center of a gripping emotion or stand off and write about the same thing with detached objectivity. She looked at people or ideas and saw them, disconcertingly, both as they are and as she wished them to be. Her love was immediate and sure. Her scorn was as quick, and it could demolish.

He preached upon "breadth" till it argued him narrow,—
The broad are too broad to define;
And of "truth" until it proclaimed him a liar,—
The truth never flaunted a sign.
Simplicity fled from his counterfeit presence
As gold the pyrites would shun.

What confusion would cover the innocent Jesus
To meet so enabled a man!

The ministerial object of her contempt is believed to
have been the Reverend John Langdon Dudley. Before he
went to the Middle West, Dudley had a church in Middle-
town, Connecticut, where he met and married Emily Dickinson's Amherst Academy and Philadelphia friend Eliza
Coleman. If he knew of the poem, Dudley must have
wished he had never inspired it. Emily Dickinson sent
a copy to Higginson.

In eight lines Emily Dickinson destroyed a pretentious
man. It took her twelve scornful lines to deflate what
she saw as the artificiality of some women.

> What soft, cherubic creatures
>   These gentlewomen are!
> One would as soon assault a plush
>   Or violate a star.
>
> Such dimity convictions,
>   A horror so refined
> Of freckled human nature,
>   Of Deity ashamed,—
>
> It's such a common glory,
>   A fisherman's degree!
> Redemption, brittle lady,
>   Be so ashamed of thee.

Like most people, Emily Dickinson was made up of
many parts. She was a palette of streaks and blobs of
color, a multicolored chaos out of which she had to create
both herself and her poetry. She was a swirl of contradictions. She had to resolve them to find herself through

her poetry. She told Higginson that women talked too much. She could not stop talking on paper. Imagine, if you can, a silent Shakespeare; articulateness was just as inherent in Emily Dickinson.

At one point she sent Higginson a poem that she evidently liked, for she sent out four other copies, to Mrs. Edward Tuckerman, the Norcross cousins, Helen Hunt Jackson, and Mabel Loomis Todd. It is one of the few poems to which she gave a title. She called it "The Humming-Bird." She might as accurately have titled it "Emily Dickinson." It has all her grace and sureness. It has her darting flight, her hovering, her pinpoint selection of the telling word or phrase, and her speed and elusiveness.

> A route of evanescence
> With a revolving wheel;
> A resonance of emerald;
> A rush of cochineal.
> And every blossom on the bush
> Adjusts its tumbled head;—
> The mail from Tunis, probably,
> An easy morning's ride.

Emily Dickinson was seldom temperate. She was an extremist. She was not interested in ecstasy, only in unbearable ecstasy. She was not interested in pain, only in agony. She spoke extravagantly because she felt extravagantly. Only extraordinary love appealed to her. It so enthralled her that she carried her idea of it even into her conception of God.

> God is a distant, stately lover,
> Woos, as He tells us, by his Son;
> Verily, a vicarious courtship,

Miles and Priscilla were such an one.
But lest the soul, like fair Priscilla,
Choose the envoy and spurn the groom;
Vouches with hypocritic archness,
Miles and John Alden are synonym.

When this poem was first published in *The Christian Register*, April 21, 1891, it aroused such a protest from the orthodox, who were horrified by its levity, that Emily Dickinson's editors felt forced to omit it from a volume of her poems then in preparation. Obviously Emily Dickinson had read Longfellow's "Courtship of Miles Standish," but she had carried her comparison too far for the pious. A sense of humor is heresy to the humorless.

Many people breathe air. Ordinarily they do not notice it too much. The stuff is around, and use of it so habitual that the act is unconscious. Occasionally they notice and say, as some did in Amherst, "It's a nice day, ain't it?" or "Feels good 'smornin'." Emily Dickinson noticed it in "I taste a liquor never brewed" and confessed to intoxication.

No one reading the poem needs to be told, as Emily Dickinson told Louise Norcross, "I was reared in the garden." She had never seen the Rhine, but she had studied geography in Amherst Academy and learned about alcohol in her Mount Holyoke chemistry class. No one had to teach her about a summer's day or her rapture in it.

Emily could share her joy in simple things. She could share her hurt. She intensified the pleasure that people feel, and she took the loneliness from the hurt.

She must habitually have said "he don't" for "he doesn't," for she wrote it that way. She never learned where to put the apostrophe in negative contractions and wrote "is'nt" for "isn't." She cared little for number or tense and used plural verbs with singular subjects or the reverse. She used the contracted pronoun and verb "it's" for the possessive pronoun "its." These things bothered Higginson, as they bothered editors like Bowles and Holland, who had gone on to found and edit *Scribner's Monthly* and then, when its name was changed, *The Century* in New York. Editors shied from these minor flaws as well as from the subtlety and originality of her work.

Yet she did get one poem, copies of which she had already sent to Higginson and Gordon Ford, published March 12, 1864. It appeared in *The Round Table*, which was edited in New York by her cousin Henry F. Sweetser.

> Some keep the Sabbath going to church;
> I keep it staying at home,
> With a bobolink for a chorister
> And an orchard for a dome.
>
> Some keep the Sabbath in surplice;
> I just wear my wings,
> And instead of tolling the bell for church,
> Our little sexton sings
>
> God preaches,—a noted clergyman,—
> And the sermon is never long;
> So instead of going to heaven at last,
> I'm going all along.

No longer a stately lover, God is a noted clergyman now. Emily Dickinson was still helplessly, if tenderly, flippant. Most sermons were too long. The blameless who insisted everyone go to church every Sunday and would not have missed a sermon themselves if it stretched from Sunday to Doomsday were shocked again. Going to heaven all along, indeed! And in an orchard of all places!

Emily Dickinson stayed at home with her bobolink and her noted clergyman. Instead, Lavinia—always in black silk and, except in winter, always with her parasol—went early and put little bouquets sent by her sister in the pews of friends.

Partly it was the white that Emily Dickinson habitually wore that gave Higginson the impression of her nunlike appearance. White was the traditional color of the virgin bride. White became her symbol. White is also all the colors of the solar spectrum. It encompasses all the other colors.

Out of comparable diversity, Emily Dickinson wrought unity. She got the single out of the many. Smoothness, clarity, and coolness are also characteristics of white. The color was her choice, and in her poetry its vibrant simplicity is her accomplishment.

13

The breach between the two Dickinson houses was partially mended and differences among their inhabitants at least temporarily forgotten when the first of the three children of Austin and Susan Gilbert Dickinson was born July 19, 1861. Emily Dickinson was delighted.

Named Edward but called at first Jacky, then Ned, but Eddy by the pleased grandfather for whom he was named, the child was unfortunately a partial invalid from birth. He was epileptic and suffered in addition from rheumatic fever. This but endeared him the more to Emily Dickinson, who appears now in the role of fond aunt.

Martha Gilbert Dickinson (Mattie), named for her mother's sister, was born five years later, November 30, 1866. As Madame Alexander E. Bianchi, she was destined to become Emily Dickinson's effusive family biographer.

To outward appearances, the Dickinson clan was at peace, but Mrs. Austin Dickinson's social ambitions, her glittering parties, her public personality alienated her more and more from the sister-in-law who had enthused about her when both of them were girls. Susan Dickinson sought out celebrities when they came to speak at Amherst College. She even courted the sons of celebrities who were Amherst students—there was no telling how useful they might become later. In one letter to her close friend and constant correspondent, Mrs. Josiah Holland, Emily Dickinson wrote with mingled irony and sadness that Austin was overcharged with care and Sue with scintillation. Admitting that it was strange praise, she was later to tell

Sue that she had taught her more about human nature than anyone else except Shakespeare.

Edward Dickinson had dropped out of politics with the breaking up of the Whig Party. He had hardly time for it. He was doing his duty to town, college, and family. He bought fast horses and prize cows, sold insurance, oats, and hay from his fields. Probably it was to please him that once a year at commencement, Emily Dickinson forsook her seclusion to appear as brilliant hostess at the annual Dickinson reception.

Then, surrounded by laughing and prattling guests—doing a little scintillating of her own—she acted her part with zest and grace, just as if entertaining guests were an ordinary event and nothing had happened to set her apart.

It was Austin Dickinson who greeted the Reverend Jonathan Leavitt Jenkins who came to Amherst in 1867 to be pastor of the First Church and, with his family, a Dickinson friend and neighbor. Quickly Jenkins pushed for a new church building, and Austin was his principal backer in the move, which caused some dissension in the congregation. The minister and his ally won, and the First Church built a new stone building on land nearly opposite Austin's house. When the new church—Neo-Gothic, high-steepled, and of Pelham granite—was dedicated in September 1868, Edward Dickinson gave the principal address.

The story is told that one evening Emily Dickinson slipped out of the house and with her brother ventured to a spot in the hedge in front of his house to see the imposing new church that Austin had championed. While it was under construction, the old meetinghouse, lecture room, and parsonage were advertised for sale in the *Hampshire Express,* inquiries to be made of Luke Sweetser or

William A. Dickinson. The Dickinsons, father and son, must have engineered the sale of the meetinghouse to Amherst College and its transformation into College Hall.

Emily Dickinson was badly frightened when her father fell ill during the winter of 1870. She called his illness "the terror of the winter." In the spring of 1871 she wrote Louise Norcross, "Father was very sick. I presumed he would die, and the sight of his lonesome face all day was harder than personal trouble. He is growing better, though, physically reluctantly. I hope I am mistaken, but I think his physical life do'nt want to live any longer. You know he never played, and the straightest engine has its leaning hour."

For one reason only did Edward Dickinson consent to run for the Massachusetts General Court in 1873. Consistently he had been a strong advocate of the railroads. Though with many others he had suffered financially through railroad failures, he believed that railroads meant prosperity for the Commonwealth and particularly for Amherst and its environs. He ran as a Republican and won his seat in the state legislature by obtaining almost two thirds of the vote cast.

As unpredictable and as willful as his daughter, the Honorable Edward Dickinson was reluctant to leave home. Everything about it had become dearer to the man of seventy-one. At Christmas just before he left for Boston he did something which his daughter noted with fondness and understanding. The day was cold, and there was snow on the ground. Fearing that the birds could not find food, Edward Dickinson went to the barn in his slippers and came back with grain, which he scattered on the ground for them. Then, as Emily Dickinson wrote, he stood back out of sight, embarrassed lest the birds recognize him as their benefactor.

When the General Court opened its session in early January 1874, the Honorable Edward Dickinson was quickly appointed to the Joint Special Committee of the Senate and the House on the Hoosac Tunnel Line of Railroads. He threw himself immediately into the fight to complete the four-and-a-half-mile tunnel under Hoosac Mountain in the northwestern corner of Massachusetts. Via the Troy & Greenfield extension of the Vermont & Massachusetts Railway, this tunnel would give Boston direct access to the upper Hudson Valley and the West. Massachusetts had granted a subsidy of two million dollars to the road in 1854 to complete the work, but almost twenty years later it was still unfinished. Rival railroads fought the construction, and boring of the tunnel had proved an almost impossible engineering feat. Attempts had killed a number of workers, and wrecked heavy machinery lay rusting at the tunnel entrance.

Edward Dickinson wrote Austin almost daily about details of their business, which Austin was conducting alone in his father's absence. He reported on his activities at the state capital, particularly about the work of the all-important committee. He was pushing in the legislature for the rights and privileges of Amherst College. He pressed successfully for the establishment in Amherst of the Massachusetts Agricultural College, which eventually became the huge University of Massachusetts.

Edward Dickinson was at home on what seems to have been the afternoon of Sunday, June 14, 1874. His wife was not present, and Vinnie was asleep. Though she usually stayed by herself, Emily preferred to be with her father that afternoon, and she saw that he was "particularly pleased" by her company. His pleasure almost embarrassed her, so when Austin came in she suggested that the two men go for a walk.

On the morning of Tuesday, June 16, a very warm day, Edward Dickinson of the Fourth Hampshire District, spoke at length in Boston in support of a bill to appropriate another three million dollars to complete the Troy & Greenfield Railway by finishing the Hoosac Tunnel. Feeling faint, he sat down. Then, accompanied by a friend, he walked back to his rooms in the Tremont House. The doctor who was summoned diagnosed an apoplectic stroke. Without knowing that his patient, now unconscious, was allergic to the drug, he administered morphine.

Emily Dickinson got the date a day early in this letter to Louise and Fannie Norcross, but she conveyed the other facts tightly as well as her tight emotions.

> We were eating our supper the fifteenth of June, and Austin came in. He had a despatch in his hand, and I saw by his face we were all lost, though I didn't know how. He said that father was very sick, and he and Vinnie meant to go. The train had already gone. While horses were dressing news came he was dead. Father does not live with us now— he lives in a new house. Though it was built in an hour it is better than this. He hasn't any garden . . . so we take him the best flowers, and if we only knew he knew, perhaps we could stop crying.

Emily Dickinson could never reconcile herself to death. The West Cemetery, which was opposite the North Pleasant Street house, was still visible behind the East Main Street mansion. The funerals came and went. People walked to place flowers on the graves. Death fascinated and repelled Emily, but her father's death was different. It was incredible, and seemed impossible.

Edward Dickinson had been fact and reality. It was as if, spent, Atlas had let the world slip from his bowed shoulders and crash to the ground. The god lay dead and the world shattered. Yet Emily Dickinson expected her father home by the next train. At least there would be a letter. She lived in his house, on his grounds. He was everywhere about her.

Not knowing how to break the news to Mrs. Dickinson, who, as so often, was unwell, the family at first tried to hide the facts of her husband's death from her. When someone inadvertently let the grim news slip, she said only, "I loved him so!"

The newspapers were filled with encomiums. In the *Republican,* Samuel Bowles called Edward Dickinson "a Chevalier Bayard, without fear, without reproach." A great crowd came to the funeral, spilling out over the lawn and into the street. The Dickinson's neighbor, the Reverend J. L. Jenkins, conducted the service. Emily Dickinson did not attend. She remained in her room with the door opened a little so that she could hear. Of all who came she spoke only to Samuel Bowles.

There was no hearse. The body of Edward Dickinson was borne across the fields to the West Cemetery. Amherst professors and leading citizens of the town were his honorary bearers. Shops were closed and all business of the village ceased during the funeral.

The next Sunday, with Mrs. Dickinson, Vinnie, and Austin included in the congregation, Pastor Jenkins preached a sermon on the death of Edward Dickinson. He compared him to the prophet Samuel. Of the many who expressed their sympathy and offered their condolences Emily Dickinson was helped most by one who said simply, "I am sorry." Once the whole of one of her letters to

Higginson had read, "Carlo died. E. Dickinson. Would you instruct me now?" She whose weapon was words knew that it was too soon for words now.

Austin was laid waste. He and his father had been together at work as well as at home ever since his return to Amherst from Harvard Law School. They had been in daily, sometimes hourly, contact. To him his father had seemed immortal. Now he was responsible morally and emotionally not only for his wife and children, but also for his mother and sisters. He had succeeded his father as treasurer of Amherst College, had worked with him in town and church affairs. Now he had wholly to take his place.

In 1876 Austin took his son Ned to see the Centennial Exposition in Philadelphia, but generally he stayed closer to Amherst than his father had done. Beautification of town and college through plantings of trees and shrubs helped assuage the loneliness he felt after his father's death and the loneliness he felt in his own home.

The effect of her father's death on Emily Dickinson was as fixed as his influence on her had been when he lived. She said she had been used to thinking of the door to his room as safety when she passed it on her way upstairs at night. Now she had to be her own safety. She was to speak later of what she called the incredible years when she had a father.

14

Emily Dickinson and Helen Maria Fiske were born in Amherst less than three months apart in 1830. They knew each other as children and as schoolgirls and presumably until Helen Fiske's marriage to Edward Bissell Hunt. The Hunts visited Amherst frequently and sometimes called at the Dickinsons'. Emily talked with the young officer and found his conversation amusing, particularly his remark that Carlo understood the law of gravitation.

Helen Hunt's marriage ended in tragedy. In 1863 Major Hunt was killed while testing an underwater device he had developed for the army. Their first son had died when less than a year old. Their second son died in April 1865.

The next year Helen Hunt returned to Newport, Rhode Island, where she had lived for a time when her husband was stationed there, and by chance the young widow took lodgings in the same boardinghouse with T. W. Higginson and his wife. Higginson was delighted with her and took her under his wing. Under his tutoring and encouragement she began to write. She was an apt student. She imitated Higginson's writings, freely acknowledged him as her literary mentor, and very quickly became a prolific writer of both prose and verse. Higginson was professionally familiar with the journalistic world, knew editors, their tastes, and what the various magazines wanted for their readers. Helen Hunt, a sound businesswoman, wrote for the market. *The Nation, The Independent,* and *Scribner's Monthly* published her work in profusion.

It was through coincidence then and through Higginson that Helen Hunt came to know about the writing of
her old schoolfellow. She read the verse that Emily Dickinson had sent to Higginson, delighted in it, and was
generous and enthusiastic in her praise.

The relationship of Helen Hunt and Emily Dickinson
has been so smudged by guesswork, by interpretations
that do not interpret, by Lavinia Dickinson, who was
never notorious for strict adherence to the literal truth,
and, unwittingly, perhaps, by Emily Dickinson herself, that
the complete story is not known. Probably it never will be
known. After her sister's death Lavinia destroyed almost
all the letters Emily Dickinson received and had retained.
Many, she said proudly, were from nationally known
persons. Helen Hunt's own papers were destroyed after
her death.

Just when the two women met in middle life is not clear,
but evidently they had met and correspondence had already been established between them well before 1875.
Seeking relief from a bronchial ailment, Helen Hunt spent
the winter of 1873–1874 in Colorado Springs. There she
met William Sharpless Jackson, banker and railway promoter. They were married in October 1875. By this time
Emily Dickinson knew her well enough to send Helen
Hunt Jackson a letter expressing her good wishes and to
enclose a poem.

The contrast between the two women was marked. One
was the unknown reclusive spinster of a rural village in
western Massachusetts. The other was a woman of the
world, twice married, traveled, successful, and popular.
It speaks much for the character of both that they were
attracted to each other. Emily Dickinson was grateful for
the praise of a highly regarded woman writer. Helen Hunt

Jackson was determined to bring her friend to the world's attention.

A partner as well as manager of the Boston publishing house of Roberts Brothers, Thomas Niles, like Higginson, was a feminist. He had a penchant for women writers, and "discovered" Louisa May Alcott when he read the letters she had written home about her experiences as a nurse in a Union army hospital in Washington. It was Niles who suggested that she write a book for girls. Louisa Alcott doubted that she could, but the triumphant result was *Little Women* and all her books that followed.

An astute publisher, Niles had quickly recognized the commercial possibilities in Helen Hunt, who signed her work only "H.H.," when she signed it at all. As a publishing maneuver Niles decided to put out what he called a No-Name series of books. Each book would be unsigned but by "A Great Unknown." The first book scheduled in the series was *Mercy Philbrick's Choice* by Helen Hunt Jackson.

The novel was about a woman poet in a New England village who was instructed by a tutor who died young. The heroine, who always dressed in white, was secretly in love with a well-known minister. When the book was successfully published, gossip said that the poetess was modeled after Emily Dickinson.

Vinnie is supposed to have said that Helen Hunt spent two weeks in the mansion in Amherst, she and Emily collaborating on a story. Emily had not done her share of the work, so vengefully Helen Hunt had betrayed her confidences and caricatured her collaborator (presumably in the Saxe Holm stories) as Mercy Philbrick. Later speculation identified the hero of the novel with the Reverend Charles Wadsworth.

Helen Hunt Jackson—Helen Hunt then—had been in Amherst in 1870, but there is no record that she stayed at the mansion or even saw Emily Dickinson at that time. She had grown up in Amherst. Naturally she used it, disguised, when she wanted a New England background for her tale. She knew that Emily Dickinson wrote poetry and probably knew from Higginson that she always dressed in white. Probably she used these as piquant details in a composite characterization drawn largely from herself, for she was a poetess too.

Far from ridiculing Emily Dickinson or violating her presumed confidences, Helen Hunt Jackson liked and admired her and was wholeheartedly intent on getting her verse published.

In August 1876 she wrote her enclosing a circular for the No-Name series and asking her to contribute to a volume of poetry to be published in it. She told Emily that she was herself to be a contributor. Emily Dickinson demurred. In October of the same year Helen Hunt Jackson was staying in Ashfield, a village in the Berkshire foothills about twenty-five miles from Amherst. She drove down and had a long talk with Emily Dickinson, who obviously wished greatly to see her, and again urged that she allow some of her poetry to appear in the book.

Emily Dickinson knew nothing of the editing and publishing world, which her friend knew thoroughly. It was a puzzling unknown, and she was suspicious of it. She wrote Higginson, telling him of Mrs. Jackson's visit and asking his advice. We do not know what he replied. Probably he backed the request of his protégée, but Emily continued a show of reluctance.

Helen Hunt Jackson honestly believed in the special qualities of her friend's poems. She knew a number of them by heart. She persisted, and finally Emily Dickinson agreed to let her include one poem in the proposed book. When *A Masque of Poets* appeared in 1878, the last poem in it, unsigned, as were all the poems in the volume, was "Success." This was one of the four poems Emily Dickinson had enclosed in her first letter to Higginson in 1862.

Emily Dickinson had wanted success when she first wrote the poem. She still wanted it. Despite the reluctance, real or assumed, with which she allowed her friend to publish the poem, she was sending others to Samuel Bowles, Josiah Holland, and to Thomas Niles.

When she wrote Niles in January 1879, thanking him for her author's copy of *A Masque of Poets,* she enclosed two of her poems. Niles replied that (as she undoubtedly knew) she was entitled to her copy of the book and told her that "Success" was generally ascribed to Ralph Waldo Emerson. That was high praise for Emily Dickinson, who remembered always that Benjamin Franklin Newton had introduced her to Emerson's poetry.

She enclosed more of her poems in later letters to Niles. In 1883 she sent him a valuable copy of the poems of "Currer, Ellis and Acton Bell" (Charlotte, Emily, and Anne Brontë). He returned it as too rare a gift for him to accept, saying in his letter of March 1883 that he would take instead, "a M.S. collection of your poems, that is if you want to give them to the world through the medium of a publisher."

A writer does not submit material to an editor—or send him a rare book—unless he is seeking publication. The truth is that Niles did not really like Emily Dickinson's poetry. As with Higginson, his tastes were conventional and of his time. A bachelor, but one of fifteen children,

Niles had had plenty of nieces and nephews to help him judge the commercial possibilities of *Little Women.* They could not gauge those of Emily Dickinson for him.

It was Helen Hunt Jackson who kept prodding Niles. His letter even contains a phrase similar to one she used when she wrote this to Emily Dickinson:

> My Dear Friend,—What portfolios full of verses you must have! It is a cruel wrong to your "day and generation" that you will not give them light.
>
> If such a thing should happen as that I should outlive you, I wish you would make me your literary legatee and executor. Surely after you are what is called "dead," you will be willing that the poor ghosts you have left behind should be cheered and pleased by your verses, will you not? You ought to be. I do not think we have a right to withhold from the world a word or a thought any more than a *deed* which might help a single soul. . . .

Emily Dickinson said that she met Mrs. Jackson only twice. She did not say her meetings with Helen Maria Fiske, whom she saw many times when they were young, or with Helen Hunt had been limited to two. Was she being evasive? She could be and often was.

15

When Emily Dickinson read the plays and poems of William Shakespeare she wondered why any other books had ever been written. All the wisdom and beauty she could conceive of were in Shakespeare. There are many allusions to him or echoes of his lines in her verse or letters. She knew Bassanio's question in *The Merchant of Venice*.

> Tell me where is fancy bred,
> Or in the heart or in the head?

She also knew the answer. With her the fancy she expressed in her poetry came from both mind and heart. She felt deeply. Her emotions were strong, sometimes shattering. She had the eagerly responsive heart.

In her own phrase, she cared for thought. As she had told Higginson, she could not conceive of the life without thought that many people seemed to live. Her mind was strong and playful. It was as nimble as

> . . . Jack, be quick,
> Jack, jump over the candlestick.

Emily Dickinson was sensitive, and she made her sensitivity exquisite by dwelling on what touched it. She pushed herself into extremes of joy and pain until she could catch them in words. She was easily hurt, and she made the hurt more painful by refining it, but she was too strong to be crushed. There is a toughness in poets, else they could not survive and write. Frail as she appeared, and often aware of too much and all at once, Emily Dickinson had a tough mind and a tough heart.

Life, anyway, goes on for those who are left after someone loved dies. Her father's death bewildered Emily Dickinson, but in a way it strengthened her. She had to be her own strength now, and she had to become head of the family of four women who lived in the mansion.

Her mother was unwell and had always been retiring. Vinnie was loyal and defiant, and had constituted herself the bristling protector of her sister's privacy, but, as Emily Dickinson well knew, she was commonplace. Vinnie did not care for thought either. Her principal concern was her army of cats—so many that the servants complained of the smell and the hairs on carpets, furniture, and clothing.

Vinnie had none of Emily Dickinson's awareness or her talent. She was more like Margaret (or Maggie) Maher, who had come from the big house of the socially prominent Boltwoods in 1869, intending to stay in the Dickinson mansion only until she obtained passage for California by way of Panama. Instead she remained until all of the family were gone. Maggie was a formidable woman, as decided as a Dickinson, and she was Vinnie's principal ally in guarding Emily from visitors she did not wish to see.

Just a year after her father's death Emily Dickinson suffered another blow. Never having been strong nervously or physically, Mrs. Dickinson was stricken. Emily Norcross Dickinson was paralyzed by a stroke and bedridden. A broken hip compounded the difficulty.

Emily Dickinson did her full share of the menial duties

that now befell her, Vinnie, and Maggie, and did them gladly. With their roles reversed, she became like a mother looking after her child, and she felt a deepened affection for the woman who had not previously seemed important in her life. She was surprised when she found a new satisfaction in attending to "the dear little wants" of the sick woman. She found a kind of fulfillment in the ordinary, for the mansion became just one more household in which middle-aged children looked after an aged parent whose mind and body were slowly deteriorating.

This was a share in the common lot. Tragedy, or what seemed tragedy to Emily Dickinson, came from another direction.

Samuel Bowles had become an impressive figure nationally. He was as much at home and as popular in Boston, New York, and Washington as in Springfield or Amherst. A famous journalist, a political force, he banged around the country covering political conventions and slashing out his strong opinions in strong language. The *Springfield Republican* grew in prestige and in profits. His large printing and binding operations did equally well. Sam Bowles was a successful and wealthy man.

Bowles was a ruthless reporter who would print anything he knew, no matter who got hurt, but he was also a fascinating dinner guest, admired for his wit and charm. He was a strong family man, devoted apparently to his wife and certainly to their ten children. His wife Mary seems to have been a little temperamental. She did not like the Dickinsons, and the Dickinsons did not like her. Early in his friendship with Austin, Bowles wrote asking that the Dickinsons know and understand Mary for what she really was rather than what she did and said.

To recuperate from numerous breakdowns resulting from his charged energy and vicious ambition, Bowles traveled widely in Europe and, more unusual at the time, in the American West. He poured his impressions into letters to the *Republican* which were later gathered into books: *Across the Continent; A Summer's Journey to the Rocky Mountains; The Switzerland of America* (Colorado); *Records of Travel Between the Mississippi and the Pacific Ocean,* and others.

Admired by his foremost colleagues—Horace Greeley in New York, Murat Halstead in Cincinnati, "Marse" Henry Watterson in Louisville—Sam Bowles, as he was usually called, was also attracted to women. He was particularly attracted to intellectual women. One of these was Maria Whitney, a distant cousin of his wife, whom he met in 1861 while convalescing in Northampton from one of his bouts of illness. Miss Whitney was of an intellectual and academic family. One brother, a linguist, taught Sanskrit at Yale; another, geology at Harvard. In 1867 Maria Whitney entered the Bowles home in Springfield as companion to Mrs. Bowles and family intimate. She left about a year later, when Mary Bowles accused her of trying to alienate her husband's affections, but Maria Whitney's relations with the Bowleses did not cease.

With Samuel Bowles paying her expenses, she accompanied his older children when they were sent to school in Europe, Bowles visiting them there. She was, as she put it, "a member of the Bowles party" on vacation trips and on trips to Washington and other cities. For five years, 1875 to 1880, she taught modern languages at Smith College, but most of the time, due largely to differences with its president, who may have disapproved of her relations to Samuel Bowles, she was abroad.

Maria Whitney was independent and unconventional. She was well aware that her situation was unusual, but did not try to conceal it or apologize for it. Emily Dickinson could sympathize and admire.

Samuel Bowles grew so seriously ill in December 1877 that his life was despaired of. His newspaper reported continually on his dangerous condition. Greatly agitated, Emily Dickinson wrote the Reverend Charles Wadsworth of a terrible new sorrow in her life. Though he did not know to what she referred, Wadsworth replied immediately in an almost formal note of pastoral sympathy. Samuel Bowles rallied but then grew worse. Not quite fifty-two years old, he died January 11, 1878.

Austin and Vinnie went to the funeral, but Emily Dickinson stayed alone in her room during the services, writing to Higginson of her new loss. She wrote Mary Bowles a letter charged with feeling, but reserved her deepest concern for Maria Whitney.

I have thought of you often since the darkness—though we cannot assist another's night. I have hoped you were saved. That he has received immortality who so often conferred it, invests it with a more sudden charm.

Austin Dickinson represented Amherst College at a memorial service for Samuel Bowles held in Springfield in February. Bowles had been a trustee of the college, and he and Austin had been close. Emily Dickinson, of course, did not go. Instead she wrote Maria Whitney again. She made clear her understanding at the same time that she tried to comfort.

Whether or not Emily Dickinson had ever actually been "in love" with Samuel Bowles is impossible to know, but certainly she had loved him and could understand only too well the emotions of a woman bereft.

Shared loss brought the two women together. There were more letters, and Emily began sending the family carriage to Northampton to bring Maria Whitney to Amherst for visits with her.

Emily Dickinson believed firmly in immortality. She knew that "Mr. Sam" was now with her father. The knowledge consoled her, but she would have preferred them both alive in this world.

She was more than ever alone, but her seclusion was never absolute. Her arbitrary and autocratic withdrawal became a fixed habit that was hard or impossible to break, but she was a recluse only physically. When Vinnie did the shopping she brought back the village gossip as well as household necessities. Austin was in and out several times a day with his news of litigation, crime, scandal, the First Church, and the college. Each year Emily Dickinson sat up all night to watch the circus pass up East Main Street from the railway station to its grounds on North Pleasant, not far above the village center.

Emily saw those she wished to see. Higginson came again when he lectured in Amherst. Helen Hunt Jackson brought her new husband for Emily Dickinson to inspect and approve. Emily Dickinson read her *Republican* every day and the numerous magazines to which the family subscribed. Vinnie and Maggie blandly told callers that Miss Emily, who, the callers knew, never left the house, was not at home. Emily was not at home to them, but she was at home for the hired men, for peddlers who came to the back door, for Gypsy and Indian women who came selling their wares. She liked them, and these simpler people did not impinge on her privacy.

Distilling the essence of her life into almost eighteen hundred poems, Emily lived in their creation, but she must have spent almost as much time and effort writing letters. The hundreds of her letters gathered and published after her death have to be but a fraction of all those she wrote, composing them as carefully as she did her verse. How many were discarded by their recipients after reading and how many lost we cannot know. When she knew that she was dying, Emily Dickinson asked that her letters be destroyed, and she had written frequently and copiously to many friends, to relatives, and to the total strangers whom the retiring woman never hesitated to approach.

Letters were mind-to-mind and heart-to-heart without the distraction, sometimes the disturbance, of physical presence between. Emily lived in these letters, which many times she wrote in drafts, correcting and recorrecting them before she sent fair copies to the post.

Before his death she wrote lighthearted, teasing letters to Samuel Bowles, though profundities sometimes crept into her "hyperbolic archness" and seriousness when she asked after his health. Many of her most characteristic and delightful letters went over many years to Elizabeth Chapin Holland. Like Bowles, the Hollands traveled widely, with Dr. Holland pouring out popular narratives and whimsical travel essays. Wherever her friends went, Emily strove to keep them close, but she also wrote to people nearer at hand, as to Mrs. Edward Tuckerman, wife of Amherst's famed professor of botany. Tuckerman's study of lichens took him on long field trips. Tuckerman's Ravine on Mount Washington in New Hampshire is named for him.

Those to whom Emily Dickinson wrote led active lives.

They traveled, had children, lectured, edited, preached, earned a living. They could not keep up with the poet, who did none of these things, or match her intensity. Emily Dickinson kept excusing herself for writing so often or writing before they had had time or a chance to answer a previous letter. Sometimes she asked plaintively why she had not heard from them.

There is an unconscious note of pleading in many of Emily's letters. She kept trying to make herself known. In her own way, she kept asking for understanding from the few who, she hoped, were capable of giving it to her. Because her letters were so much of her life, she was almost insistent. Once Emily Dickinson's soul had elected you, there was no escape.

She wrote Elizabeth Chapin Holland, who suffered removal of an infected eye in Berlin, as woman to woman, but even here she was often evasive and enigmatic, as if she could not bring herself to full self-revelation. She wrote fond and homely letters to Fanny and Louise Norcross. She often puzzled Thomas Wentworth Higginson in her letters. When he made his second visit to the mansion, she told him that, at any rate, one could always be grateful that one was oneself, and puzzled him again. Often Emily Dickinson's letters must have confused even those who loved her, wanted to understand, and longed, if they could, to help her.

Not all of Emily Dickinson's continual correspondence went through the mails. To friends among the Amherst families that the Dickinsons recognized she sent notes with gifts of flowers, jellies, or bread or cake that she had baked. The note might be folded by her deft fingers into the cup of a flower. It might be a poem or it might be an impish quip.

Though unseen, she was punctilious about her social obligations. She sent get-well notes, thank-you notes, and sympathy notes by the score. She paid the little "attentions," as Amherst called them, of flowers or other small gifts that were expected in polite village society. Among all else that she was, the many-sided Emily Dickinson was very much the lady. In the eyes of those who did not really know her she might seem an eccentric, but even they knew that Emily Elizabeth Dickinson was, by birth, upbringing, and inherent courtesy, a gentlewoman in a genteel college town.

She sent a breathless note to Susan Gilbert Dickinson in early August 1875. Signed "Sister," it expressed her joy at the change in the domestic fortunes of the Dickinsons and what it promised.

The third and last child of Susan and Austin Dickinson was born August 1, 1875, and named Thomas Gilbert. In the midst of death and illness here was new life, new hope. Austin and his wife were drawn together, at least for a time. The increasing bitterness and sometimes open warfare between Susan Dickinson and Vinnie was halted by a truce. Emily Dickinson was elated.

16

Gilbert, or Gib—for his first given name was never used —was a delightful child, healthy, good-natured, and attractive. With him, more than with the older Ned and Mattie, Emily Dickinson was from the first the adoring maiden aunt. As soon as she had one, she sent his baby picture to Helen Hunt Jackson. Mrs. Jackson replied in a cordial letter, but other people's children are seldom fascinating to outsiders. She wrote that she presumed the picture was of Emily's brother's child.

Emily Dickinson loved the baby. She treasured the bright sayings of the small child when he was a little older. She was delighted that when Gilbert was accused by Vinnie of chasing one of her cats (Emily Dickinson always wrote "Pussy"), Gilbert argued that the cat had been chasing itself. Happily and proudly Emily Dickinson watched her small nephew develop and was as admiring as everyone else when he could show his mastery of the small tricycle he had learned to ride.

Gilbert became the smallest of the troupe of children who played about the lawns of the two houses. There were Austin's three, "Did" and "Mac," children of the ministerial Jenkinses across the street, and a few others. Emily Dickinson watched the children as they raced about and, though often unseen, became their companion and fellow conspirator.

She did not play tag or hide-and-seek with them, but Emily, as she called herself in talk with them, was there aiding and abetting in their games and fancies. She made a game of lowering cake and cookies to them in a basket dangled on a string from her upstairs room. Mary Adele Allen, who was one of the children who played in the Dickinson yard, remembers her at other times eagerly handing cookies out to them through the half-opened shutters of the pantry.

The children were Emily Dickinson's messengers, running her notes to Susan Dickinson, Mrs. Jenkins, and other of her friends. She was party to all the children's schemes. When they decided to publish and circulate a hand-lettered neighborhood newspaper, Emily became a charter subscriber and a contributor to the first and only issue that appeared. Once when the children were playing inside the mansion, with Emily Dickinson encouraging in the background, she told them that if anyone else, even the butcher's boy, appeared, she would jump into the flour barrel. They hoped the butcher's boy would come. Emily upside down and covered with flour in a barrel was something they wanted to see.

She wrote light verses for Gilbert. She gave or sent him little presents. Once she gave him a potted plant to take to his teacher.

It was in her garden that the children saw her most often. There, among her lemon verbena, jockey club, roses, sweet clover, star-of-Bethlehem, heliotrope, and great clumps of day lilies, she told them about flowers. Working on a rug spread for her on the grass, she potted plants for the conservatory off the dining room, which gave her flowers throughout the New England winter. She liked the bulb plants best and always planted perennials in her garden. They came up year after year in annual resurrection. There was immortality in that.

Austin Dickinson had always shared his sister's love of

nature. With his life concentrated in Amherst, more and more his greatest interest outside the law became the beautification of the village. The leader of what was first Amherst's Ornamental Tree Association, then the Village Improvement Society, he delighted in driving through the Pelham Hills and into the rough nearby country in search of fine young trees and shrubs that could be transplanted to the Amherst Common, to spots about the college buildings, or to his own grounds.

It was in the fall of 1878 that Helen Hunt Jackson brought her husband to meet Emily Dickinson. They talked of Samuel Bowles, his widow, Maria Whitney, and many other things, but it is unlikely that Emily Dickinson told them or any of her other friends about what must have been uppermost in her mind.

In her late forties Emily Dickinson was deeply and happily in love.

She had known State Supreme Court Justice Otis Phillips Lord since her childhood. While her father lived, Lord and his wife were frequent visitors to the mansion. In 1869 Amherst College made him an honorary doctor of laws, for this son of the college was one of the best-known public figures in Massachusetts. The Lords continued their visits to Amherst, staying for weeks at a time at Amherst House and calling both at the mansion and at Austin's. In 1877, when Otis Lord was sixty-five years old, Elizabeth Lord died. Two of his wife's nieces kept the Salem house for him. They came with him on more visits to Amherst, Lord spending much of his time with Emily Dickinson.

Just when Lord and Emily Dickinson fell in love is not known. Whether he offered marriage is not known. It has been suggested that he did but that the nieces, friends of Sue's, objected. It has also been suggested that Emily Dickinson knew it was too late to change her way of life.

In some unexplained way Emily Dickinson's letters to Judge Lord came into the possession of Austin. He gave them to the first editor of his sister's verse, but most were not published until seventy years after Emily Dickinson's death. They are the devoted letters of a woman in love who knows that her love is returned. The earliest was written in 1878.

It is rhapsodic, exultant, and unrestrained. She thanks God for her "lovely Salem," calling Lord by the name of his own as if he were a lord of the realm, for even here she must play with words. She begs Lord to save her from worshiping him as a god. She fears the fierceness of such love would crush them both. The letters are almost painful to read.

There are many of these love letters. Some have the tone and almost the rhythm of the Song of Solomon. Lord continued to come to Amherst. He was there in April 1882. The next month Vinnie, after talking with Austin, who was on his way down the hill to the railway station, came in and asked Emily whether she had seen anything in the newspaper that morning that concerned them. Emily said No. Vinnie then told her that Judge Lord was seriously ill. In a well-known letter Emily Dickinson wrote her beloved of her shock and terror at the news. Panic gripped her. Her sight blurred. She felt as if she were freezing. For support she clutched at a chair that seemed moving past, then abandoned it to run to the hired man as he entered the kitchen and sob her heart out against his blue jacket as he tried to comfort her.

Judge Lord recovered, and Emily Dickinson could be at peace again. Her love was full devotion, self-abnegation, humble. There was more of Emily Norcross Dickinson in her, perhaps, than either mother or daughter realized.

After a long illness and invalidism their mother died in November 1882, leaving a hole in the days of Emily and Lavinia Dickinson. They grieved, but it was her father Emily Dickinson remembered continually. Once to comfort someone where there had been a death in the family she wrote only, "I had a father once."

In December Judge Lord asked her to his home in Salem. Emily Dickinson said that he had "called her to his breast." On the first Sunday of that month she wrote that the others had gone to church but that she was in church at home—not this time with God preaching and a bobolink for a chorister but with her thoughts of him.

Emily Dickinson was in love with Otis Lord when, in 1880, she had an unexpected visitor. Vinnie called to tell her that the man with the deep voice wanted to see her. It was the Reverend Charles Wadsworth. He said there had been no time to let her know, as he had stepped from his pulpit to the train. When she asked, "How long?" he answered with what Emily Dickinson called a roguish smile, "Twenty years!" At one point during what must have been their excited talk he told her that he might die at any time, but his light comment seems to have made no deep impression then.

Dr. Josiah Holland died October 12, 1881. Another of her father's friends who had been her friend and who, it is likely, she hoped would be her editor, was gone. To a telegram from his family she answered, "We read the words, but we know them not." She tried to comfort Elizabeth Holland—but asked for details of Holland's death.

To her Norcross cousins she wrote, "Did the little sisters know that Dr. Holland had died—the dark man with the doll wife, whom they used to see at 'Uncle Edward's'?"

The Reverend Charles Wadsworth died of pneumonia, April 1, 1882. When Vinnie saw a newspaper notice and told Emily of it, she discovered that her sister had known of Wadsworth's death for ten days but had said nothing about it. The silence was a measure of her hurt. She immediately began a long correspondence with a Brooklyn friend of Wadsworth's. She asked about the minister's tastes and his personal life, of which she knew nothing, and explained with typical exaggeration that Wadsworth had been her "shepherd since little Girlhood." James Dickson Clark sent her another volume of Wadsworth's sermons and a picture of Wadsworth which she hung in her room. (It is there now.)

Her father, Bowles, her mother, Holland, Wadsworth. It must have seemed to Emily Dickinson as if the world she knew and loved was being wrest from her piece by piece. Soon there was much worse.

Toward the end of September 1883, eight-year-old Gilbert Dickinson grew suddenly and violently ill after playing in a stream with another small boy. His mother and father were up with him most of the night. His condition grew worse. It was typhoid fever. By Thursday, October 4, indicated as the day of crisis, little hope was held out for his recovery. Thomas Gilbert Dickinson died at a quarter of five that next afternoon.

That night, for the first time in fifteen years, Emily Dickinson went through the hedge and across the lawns to Austin's house. She stayed a long time, but choking emotion and the odor from the disinfectants that had been used in the sickroom made her violently ill. About three o'clock in the morning she stumbled home and went to bed with a blinding headache.

Handsome, bright, a favorite with adults as well as with the other children, Gilbert Dickinson had been the hope of the family. He had been generally loved, particularly by his father. The young woman who came to know Austin Dickinson best said that Austin almost died too. He was as pale as death. Gilbert had been his idol and, in her words, the only thing in his house that he cared for or that really loved him. The Reverend Jonathan Jenkins, pastor now of a church in Pittsfield, but Austin's friend and neighbor, who had known Gib as the playmate of his own children, conducted the funeral service.

Life was temporal, even for loved children. Emily nearly collapsed. She sent broken-hearted messages to Susan Dickinson and at least three long elegiac poems commemorating the dead child. One thinks of Emerson's "Threnody" for Waldo, the "hyacinthine boy" whom he lost when Waldo was only five.

Emily Dickinson could not forget Gilbert any more than Emerson could forget Waldo. Long afterward she talked of him and wrote of him in her letters. Her spirits and health were slow to return. Life was temporal, but poetry was lasting. She clung to it, for poetry was life. Sometimes it expressed her bitterness.

The last words in a letter which Otis Lord wrote Emily Dickinson early in March 1884 were "a caller comes." March 13, 1884, aged seventy-two, he too died, of a stroke.

Her closest friends sent understanding notes of sympathy to Emily Dickinson. She responded mechanically. In one letter she wrote, "Thank you, dears, for the sympathy. I hardly dare to know that I have lost another friend, but anguish finds it out." Anguish bit into her so deeply that in June 1884 she did collapse.

When she could, she wrote Louise and Fanny Norcross:

Eight Saturdays ago, I was making a loaf of cake with Maggie when I saw a great darkness coming and knew no more until late at night. I woke to find Austin and Vinnie and a strange physician bending over me, and supposed I was dying or had died, all was so kind and hallowed. I had fainted and lain unconscious for the first time in my life. Then I grew very sick and gave the others much alarm, but am now staying. The doctor calls it "revenge of the nerves" —but who but Death had wronged them?

It was nervous prostration, severe and of long duration. Emily Dickinson spent the entire summer of 1884 in a chair, though she continued to write both her verse and her letters.

17

In 1881 David Peck Todd, Amherst class of 1875, was hired from the United States Naval Observatory as instructor in astronomy and director of the observatory of Amherst College. With him he brought fresh from Washington society his attractive young wife. Mabel Loomis Todd had studied at the Boston Conservatory of Music. She was twenty-four, intelligent, literate, and talented. The Todds lived first in a tall old house on Deke Hill behind the mansion, then built a cottage across East Main Street on land abutting Dickinson property.

Susan Dickinson was quick to take up the young couple and make much of them. She particularly courted Mabel Todd. At first the young woman was completely captivated, and wrote her mother rapturously that Mrs. Dickinson was wonderful. They appreciated each other completely. She said that the Austin Dickinson home was her refuge in Amherst and that she played and sang for Sue for hours.

Susan Dickinson showed Mabel Loomis Todd some of Emily Dickinson's poetry, and Mrs. Todd soon learned something about the unseen woman in the big house whom she had heard people in Amherst call "The Myth."

Mabel Todd admired Susan Dickinson, but she admired Austin even more. She noted in her journal in September 1882 that "dear Mr. Dickinson . . is very fond of me" and said it was one of the proudest moments of her life when deep-voiced Austin told her that she had more ideas of which he approved than any other person he had ever met.

She confessed that she admired him extravagantly. Austin told her that he had suffered greatly all his life from sensitiveness. "He is in almost every particular my ideal man."

At Austin's she met Vinnie, and Vinnie asked her to come to the mansion to play and sing for their bedridden mother, who could hear from her room. Mabel Todd knew that the unseen Emily Dickinson would also hear. The idea fascinated her. She was fascinated the more when she received an exquisite bouquet of hyacinths, heliotrope, and some yellow flowers she could not identify with a note from Emily Dickinson.

Mabel Loomis Todd was to become very popular in Amherst. She taught music and painting in a private girls' school. She became the leading lady in amateur theatricals, sang in the First Church choir, helped her husband with his texts and reports on astronomy. She worked enthusiastically with Austin Dickinson in his civic landscape gardening, often driving with him into the hills in search of choice trees and shrubs.

When she returned from a visit to her parents in Washington in 1883, she found that her love affair with Susan Dickinson was over. Mabel Loomis Todd had anyway revised her estimate of the other's character, saying she had found startling aspects of it that she had not at first suspected. Susan was as cold and distant now as she had been warm and welcoming before. It was clear to her, of course, that Austin and Mrs. Todd were mutually attracted. The two women talked over their differences and smoothed things over, but soon there was another break in their relationship, which led to a lasting estrangement.

One incident that may well have startled her and led to her reappraisal of Susan Dickinson had occurred earlier.

When Mabel Loomis Todd told Sue that Lavinia had invited her and her husband to the mansion, Sue exclaimed that she hoped she would never allow her husband to go there. Asked why, Sue said that neither Lavinia nor Emily Dickinson had the slightest idea of morality. She improved the story by adding that she had once surprised Emily in the drawing room lying in the arms of a man.

Mabel Loomis Todd, who already suspected the other's veracity, was more than ever determined to go. She did go, and the Todds became frequent visitors. David Todd ran errands for Lavinia and acted as her escort when she made calls. He kept the Dickinson clocks in running order. Mabel Todd sang and played Bach, Beethoven, and Scarlatti while Emily Dickinson listened from the darkened hall. Mrs. Todd seldom saw more than the glow of her white dress as they talked through a partly opened door. The half-seen woman was extravagant in her praise of the music, and Mrs. Todd said she became very familiar with Emily's voice, "its vaguely surprised note dominant." Emily Dickinson sent her gifts of flowers and poems and many warmly appreciative notes. Because she knew it was a favorite flower, Mabel Todd painted a panel of Indian pipes, which so delighted Emily Dickinson that she hung it in her room.

Like Helen Hunt Jackson, whom the much younger woman resembled in her capability, her outgoing nature, generosity, and insight, Mabel Loomis Todd from the first placed a high value on Emily Dickinson's poetry.

Emily Dickinson and Helen Hunt Jackson were in frequent touch by letter, and Emily sent her many of her poems. Sometimes Mrs. Jackson asked what a line or a word meant, but insisted on return of the questioned verse and tried again and again to persuade Emily Dickinson to publish. The two women were so close in the public mind that newspaper stories still claimed that together they had written some stories, signed "Saxe Holm" that had appeared in *Scribner's*.

Helen Hunt Jackson was not well. She was suffering from nervous exhaustion when in Colorado she fell down a flight of stairs and broke her leg. Emily Dickinson sent a quick note of sympathy. Mrs. Jackson, on crutches for months and slow to recover from both illness and injury, wrote a cheerful reply. The other described her own nervous prostration and sent more of her verse.

Helen Hunt Jackson did not, as she had once suggested, outlive her friend. Aged fifty-four, she died in San Francisco, August 12, 1885. Emily Dickinson was "unspeakably shocked." Those were her words to Higginson when she learned of the death.

Immediately she wrote a letter of sympathy to William Sharpless Jackson. Then, as was her habit, she wrote to the one who was close to a lost friend, asking for the death details. This time it was Thomas Niles, to whom she had written often after publication of *A Masque of Poets*. Niles told her that Helen Hunt Jackson had died of cancer of the stomach and sent her a photograph of the woman who had done her best to help. Emily Dickinson also wrote the Reverend F. E. Emerson of Newport, a Jackson friend, asking to know "any circumstance of her life's close."

Emily Dickinson was never well after the series of deaths that struck her down. Even before her nervous prostration, "Helen of Colorado" had written worriedly of her pallor and frailty, of her wisplike hands. It was weakness of the body, not of the mind. She was as alert and as curious as ever, almost feverishly vital. She wrote little verse now but many letters, although she could write only in pencil. The letters were short, almost spasmodic in style, and filled with single-sentence paragraphs of obscure aphorisms.

Besides the letters, she sent on numerous occasions from her sickroom—Vinnie or Maggie posting them—small packets to Roswell Smith at the Century Company. She knew that Smith had been Dr. Holland's partner in founding both *Scribner's* and then the *Century*. Smith was a publisher and a promoter, not an editor, but, innocent of literary commerce, Emily Dickinson would not have understood the distinction. Holland had told Emily Fowler Ford that he found the poems she submitted to him beautiful but too rootless and ethereal for him to risk publication. In all probability, Emily Dickinson hoped that Smith —who was really a go-getting advertising man—would be more sympathetic to her work.

In an essential if odd way, Mabel Loomis Todd took Helen Hunt Jackson's place in her concern for Emily Dickinson both as a woman and as a poet. She was often in the Dickinson home, sitting with Vinnie by the fire, chatting and visiting as they both listened for any sound from the sickroom upstairs, for Vinnie and Maggie had another patient to look after now. Thin, intense, Vinnie was tigerish in her protection of her sister, and outspoken in her dislike of Susan Dickinson next door.

By November 1885 Emily Dickinson was so ill that she was forced to remain in bed. She suffered recurring bouts of particular severity followed by brief periods of what seemed to be partial recovery and convalescence. She was very ill in January 1886 but recovered enough to go on with her correspondence. She spoke simply when she wrote her Norcross cousins in March.

I scarcely know where to begin, but love is always a safe

place. I have twice been very sick, dears, with a little recess of convalescence, then to be more sick. I have been in bed since November, many years for me. . . .

Vinnie would have written, but could not leave my side. Maggie gives her love. Mine more sweetly still.

Emily

Austin sat with her many evenings. He loved his sister, and the mansion was his sanctuary from his own divided home. On one side were his wife, Mattie, and Ned. On the other he stood alone. The friction between his wife and Vinnie increased. Susan Dickinson and her children no longer spoke to the Todds.

By April 1886 Emily Dickinson had recovered enough, as she put it, to roam about her room a little. The respite was brief. She wrote another letter, her last, to Louise and Fanny Norcross. In its entirety it read:

Little Cousins,—Called back.
Emily

In the forenoon of May 13, 1886, Emily Dickinson lost consciousness. She had Bright's disease. The doctors called the new attack apoplexy. Breathing heavily and continually weakening, she remained in a coma. She was still unconscious when Mrs. Todd and her small daughter Millicent called the next evening. By the morning of Saturday May 15 all knew that, in Austin's phrase, Emily Dickinson "would not wake again this side." Emily Dickinson died before six o'clock that evening. Pitifully, Austin wrote in his diary, "I was near by."

Wednesday, May 19, was a beautiful spring day. The white casket was covered with violets and ground pine. Vinnie put two heliotrope blossoms into Emily Dickinson's hands "to take to Judge Lord." The Reverend George Dickerman, now minister of the First Church, conducted the simple service. The Reverend Jonathan Jenkins came from Pittsfield to offer the prayer. Thomas Wentworth Higginson read Emily Brontë's poem on immortality, "No coward soul is mine."

Then, according to Emily Dickinson's wish, she was carried out the back door of the mansion past the big barn with its horses, cow, and swallows and across the fields in which bright buttercups sparkled in the sun to the West Cemetery. Her bearers were not the eminent of the town and college. They were workmen who were or had been Dickinson servants or who had labored about the place. These were men Emily Dickinson knew, liked, and trusted.

Small Millicent Todd did not go to the funeral with her parents, but she watched from the field. What she most clearly remembered years later was how small the casket was.

Enclosed by a wrought-iron fence erected in 1858, the Dickinson family plot in the West Cemetery is small and modest, one tall cedar its only ornament. Side by side there are four upright stone slabs. One of the two larger ones is for Samuel Fowler Dickinson and his wife Lucretia Gunn; the other, for Edward and Emily Norcross Dickinson. The matching smaller stones are for Lavinia and Emily, who lies between her sister and her parents. The other stones bear only the names and the dates of birth and death. That for Emily Dickinson (not the original stone) is a little different.

Born, Dec. 10, 1830

CALLED BACK

May 15, 1886

18

As well as asking friends to destroy her letters, Emily Dickinson had instructed Lavinia to destroy her letters and papers, and Vinnie followed directions unquestioningly. As she told Mrs. Todd, she burned hundreds of letters, many of them from prominent people. It was when in her rummaging she came on a locked box filled with Emily Dickinson's poems, carefully copied out and tied into small packets with green and white string, that she hesitated.

Much has been made of Lavinia's amazement at the discovery. It has never seemed credible. Everyone who knew Emily Dickinson or knew of her knew that she wrote poetry. She had sent copies of more than three hundred of them to Susan Dickinson alone. She had enclosed poems in letters to a score of correspondents. She seems to have submitted them to editors and publishers. Unless she had destroyed them herself, they had to be somewhere.

Fortunately, Lavinia Dickinson stopped short. Emily had left no specific instructions that her poetry was to be destroyed. Animosities forgotten in the light of her discovery, Vinnie gathered up the packets and took them to Susan Dickinson, begging her help in getting the poems published or, as she called it, printed.

Susan Dickinson held the poems, about seven hundred of them, for a year. She had had about enough of the Dickinsons, particularly the difficult Vinnie. The family kept up a formal front for inquisitive and gossiping

Amherst, but Susan and Austin Dickinson were virtually estranged. She and Emily had managed to maintain at least the appearance of a long-vanished friendship, but she had put up with Emily's vagaries for a long time. Whether Emily Dickinson's verse was or was not real poetry Susan probably did not know, and she was really no more conversant with publishing than Vinnie. She did nothing.

More than ever determined, Lavinia now approached Mabel Loomis Todd. Always secretive and devious, her peculiarities of character and appearance more marked as she aged, she seems to have said nothing at first of having already approached Susan Dickinson. She took the packets to Mrs. Todd and begged, almost demanded, that she get the poems printed. Lavinia Dickinson knew less than any of them about the quality, or the lack of it, in her sister's work. She assumed that all that had to be done was to take the manuscript poems to some printer.

Emily Dickinson's long-deferred career as a poet and the fame for which she had once hungered can be said to have begun with her death. She was fortunate now. Mabel Loomis Todd was immersed in work with her husband and in town and college activities, but she took on eagerly what she saw would be the difficult task of editing Emily Dickinson's poems.

She and her husband examined and carefully numbered the volumes, as Lavinia called them, or the fascicles, as they began to call them. It was a job requiring patience, accuracy, and discrimination. Emily Dickinson's handwriting was difficult to decipher. She had used dashes instead of conventional punctuation and had capitalized nouns as she pleased. Some of the poems were finished pieces. Others were tentative. Many were in drafts with corrections and with substitute or alternative words or phrases added.

As Mabel Loomis Todd copied out the poems, she returned the packets to Lavinia. Vinnie kept bringing her more poems as she discovered them. Some of them were on scraps of paper or on the backs of envelopes or recipes. Also, refusing to take No for an answer, Lavinia Dickinson, now enlisted the sponsorship and coeditorship of Thomas Wentworth Higginson, because she knew that her sister had depended upon his literary advice.

Higginson went over the copies Mrs. Todd made, gave titles to many of the poems, and smoothed out rhymes by changing a word here and there. He has often been blamed for this, but for the time and under the circumstances Higginson was right. He knew the marketplace and public taste, what editors would consider and what they would summarily dismiss. Neither editors nor readers would accept poetry that was too radically different from that to which they were accustomed. Emily Dickinson was different enough in the first place.

Among his other literary or writing-connected activities, Higginson was a manuscript reader for one of the oldest and most respected Boston publishers. He tried to interest its editors in a selection of Emily Dickinson's poems. They would have none of them.

Then, because she knew that Emily Dickinson and Thomas Niles had corresponded for years and that Niles knew her verse, Mabel Loomis Todd approached Roberts Brothers. Niles was a businessman. He doubted the commercial value of Emily Dickinson's work, but he was willing to go partway with safety. He agreed to risk publication only if Lavinia Dickinson would bear the major part of the expense involved.

Knowing that the book was under way and that publication was ensured, Higginson undertook carefully planned advance publicity. To pave the way for the book and to introduce Emily Dickinson as a poet, he wrote an article for the *Christian Union* of November 12, 1890. After the book had been published, he followed this article with another in an 1891 *Atlantic* issue, in which he described his meetings with Emily Dickinson and quoted passages from her letters to him and a number of her poems.

Poems by Emily Dickinson, Edited by Two of Her Friends, Mabel Loomis Todd and T. W. Higginson, was published in Boston by Roberts Brothers in November 1890. In a brief preface Higginson told something of Emily Dickinson's life, said that she had written without thought of publication, and that "this selection from her poems is published to meet the desire of her personal friends, and especially of her surviving sister."

The small book carried on its cover a reproduction of the Indian pipes that Mrs. Todd had painted. It contained only 115 of the Dickinson poems, but many of her best. Its critical reception was varied. Some reviewers spoke glowingly of the poems while others ridiculed them; as usual, most of them hedged. Higginson and Mrs. Todd went on circuit, speaking to women's clubs, to literary societies, anywhere they could find an audience. Emily Dickinson was no longer unknown. She was a publicized literary discovery, and enough of the public went out and bought the book so that it moved quickly into new editions.

Niles forgot his timidity. There was money to be made here. Higginson changed his mind too. He saw that it would not be necessary to make any real changes in the poems for a new collection already planned. Only a year later *Poems by Emily Dickinson, Second Series* was published. This time Higginson's name preceded that of Mabel Loomis Todd, but Mrs. Todd, who had done most of the editing, wrote a longer preface than the first volume had contained.

It opens, of course, with the standard statement that the first book had been so eagerly received that a second volume of the poems was needed. Mrs. Todd spoke of the difficulties encountered in editing, of the changing Dickinson handwriting, which added to the difficulties, and of the condition of the manuscript poems. "While most of the poems bear evidence of having been thrown off at white heat, still more had received thoughtful revision. There is the frequent addition of rather perplexing foot-notes, affording large choice of words and phrases."

In her cogent appraisal, Mrs. Todd wrote, "Emily Dickinson scrutinized everything with clear-eyed frankness." She spoke of the poet's candor and lack of prejudice. Then she said, "She was not an invalid, and she lived in seclusion from no love-disappointment." Fascinated by what they had heard of Emily Dickinson's life and struck forcibly by her love poetry, readers could not believe this. Biographers as well as readers have refused to believe it since. It would spoil the story.

Public interest in Emily Dickinson and her life had been so aroused that, with the determined Lavinia helping and Niles encouraging, Mabel Loomis Todd, gathered together all the available letters. These letters were published in two volumes in 1894 as *Letters of Emily Dickinson*. Higginson was now in his seventies, but Mabel Loomis Todd was only in her early thirties. Thus she alone undertook the editing of a third volume of Emily

Dickinson's poetry. Though engrossed in the work, she was not able to complete it until she returned from an extended trip to Japan with her husband, who was sent there to observe an eclipse. Mrs. Todd stayed faithfully with the Dickinson text this time, copying exactly from the manuscripts, choosing one when several alternative words were offered, and using standard punctuation instead of Emily Dickinson's dashes.

Poems by Emily Dickinson, Third Series, edited by Mabel Loomis Todd, was published by Roberts Brothers in 1896. Mrs. Todd continued with the work in preparation for publishing a fourth volume.

Then ensued the tragicomedy which prevented publication of more of Emily Dickinson's verse until 1914.

Her impresarios as well as her devoted editors, Higginson and Mabel Loomis Todd received little reward for their long hard work on the literary remains of Emily Elizabeth Dickinson. By contract, royalties from the books went to Lavinia, who had paid most of the cost of their publication. She was to remunerate the editors through her bounty. It was not much. Triumphant at having achieved her end and basking in the fame now accruing to her sister, Vinnie felt that she had bestowed a favor on the editors instead of having received their willing help. According to Millicent Todd Bingham, Lavinia Dickinson awarded her mother a total of just two hundred dollars, Higginson about the same.

Lavinia, who knew that both Higginson and Mrs. Todd were receiving small sums from their continual lecturing and writing about Emily Dickinson, evidently considered this adequate compensation. Austin Dickinson felt differently. Moved possibly by additional sentiments, but feeling that she well deserved more substantial recognition for her work on the four books, he deeded to Mabel Loomis Todd a fifty-three-foot strip of Dickinson meadow that adjoined the Todd property.

It was a pretty expanse, which Emily Dickinson had been able to see from her upstairs room and on which Austin had lavished loving care in planting. The land was part of the Dickinson patrimony, thus the deed of transfer needed Lavinia Dickinson's signature. Jealous of her star role and resentful of the spotlight on any of the other actors in introducing Emily Dickinson, she demurred, agreed to sign, demurred again, but finally signed. Valued at from six to eight hundred dollars, the land might then have passed smoothly to Mabel Loomis Todd, who was greatly pleased.

It did not. Jealousies, acrimonies, gossip were all running high again. While some were elated, others were incensed at the new fame and growing popularity of Emily Dickinson. Susan Dickinson now claimed all property rights in poems of which Emily Dickinson had sent her copies. Lavinia Dickinson, eccentric in habit, grotesque in appearance, smelling of the cats with which she surrounded herself, grew more difficult with success. Bitterly she said that Susan Dickinson's cruelties had shortened Emily's life by ten years.

With Emily gone, Austin Dickinson's old home was no longer a refuge for him. He found another at the Todds', both David Todd and his wife helping him with his college accounts. He said that Lavinia was tricky and unreliable, had always been. Lavinia even quarreled with Susan Dickinson over the use of a manure pile used to fertilize what had been Emily Dickinson's garden.

Suspicions, recriminations, and simple hatred boiled, yet the meadow still might have gone from the Dickinsons to the Todds had Austin not been taken seriously ill in July 1895. A specialist was summoned from Boston. He determined that Austin's heart was malfunctioning. Two nurses were brought in. For several weeks Austin lay breathing hard, sometimes a little better, more often worse. William Austin Dickinson died early in the evening of August 16, 1895.

Alone now except for Maggie Maher, Lavinia Dickinson was desolate. Friendly communication with Austin's family was an impossibility. She turned more than ever to the Todds, who had been neighbors now for some fifteen years. They looked in on her frequently to make sure the older woman was all right, ran errands for her in the village and even in Boston. Vinnie often sent notes asking Mabel Todd to come to see her about this or that small practical matter that had nothing to do with the editing of Emily Dickinson's poems. One of the last things the Todds did in April 1896 was to say good-bye to Lavinia before they left for Japan.

As soon as they returned, October 14, Mabel Loomis Todd ran over to the mansion. Vinnie greeted her effusively and exclaimed with pleasure over a gift of blue china brought her from Japan.

November 16, 1896, Lavinia Norcross Dickinson filed a bill of complaint against David Peck Todd and Mabel Loomis Todd. In this legal action she claimed that fraud and misrepresentation had been used in getting her to sign the deed to the strip of Dickinson meadow and asked that the deed to it be declared null and void.

The Todds were aghast. Amherst was delighted. The Todd-Dickinson conflict gave the village something to talk about all through the long winter and something to look forward to. The vindictive crowed that they had known all along that something like this would happen. It served them all right. What Vinnie felt no one knows, but she put on a marvelous performance when the case finally came to trial March 1, 1898.

All legal right was on the side of the Todds, but Yankee-land does not approve giving away real estate, particularly when it is part of a family estate. In a blue flannel dress with bright-yellow shoes and wearing a long mourning veil, Lavinia played the part of the aged woman innocent of all of the machinations of business. In court she did not hear what she did not wish to hear. She parried questions. She forgot pertinent facts. In the admiring Yankee phrase, Vinnie had all her buttons, but she had always buttoned them as she chose. After Emily Dickinson's death and then Austin's she really did not seem to know what to do with them.

That hardly mattered. The Dickinsons were an old and respected family and, in the eyes of the righteous, its surviving member was the innocent victim of duplicity. By New England standards, the Todds were newcomers, foreigners from wicked Washington and, Lavinia's partisans hinted darkly, not everything they ought to be. They did not have a chance in Northampton. The court found for the plaintiff, and the shocked defendants were ordered to give back the disputed land. The State Supreme Court to which appeal was made sustained the verdict.

The Todds moved to Observatory House, built by the college some distance from East Main Street. Thus they were away from the mansion and the other house. All relationship between Todds and Dickinsons ceased. Work on the projected fourth volume of Emily Dickinson's poems stopped. Within months Lavinia Dickinson sold the land she had regained. Ned Dickinson, the semi-invalid son of Austin and Susan Dickinson, died, aged 39, May 3, 1899. Little more than three months later, August 31, 1899, Lavinia Dickinson died of a heart ailment.

The real victim of the family bickering was Emily Dickinson. Fifteen years passed before more of her poetry was brought out. Then, in 1914, Martha Dickinson Bianchi published *The Single Hound,* the poems that Emily Dickinson had sent her mother Susan. They were advertised as having been withheld from publication by her sister Lavinia. That was not quite accurate, but it was effective publisher's promotion.

Ten years later Martha Dickinson Bianchi published *The Life and Letters of Emily Dickinson.* The "life" was romanticized, and the letters were those that had first been published in 1894. Then came the spate: *The Complete Poems of Emily Dickinson,* 1924; *Further Poems,* 1929; *Unpublished Poems,* 1936. Various books of varying content and quality about Emily Dickinson were hurriedly published.

This was commercial exploitation of a profitable market. In some of the collections, fragments and very minor poems were mixed with more important work. Changes were made in some poems to conform with assumed critical and reader taste. The public was confused, and many readers grew cynical. How many more Dickinson poems would be discovered or concocted?

Mabel Loomis Todd spent a busy life writing, lecturing, and traveling with her husband, whose scientific pursuits took them to distant parts of the globe. Her later years she spent in Florida, but she died at her summer home on Hog Island, Maine, in 1932. Her daughter Millicent Todd Bingham took up the work where her mother had dropped it and in 1945 published, as edited by mother and daughter, *Bolts of Melody*. This collection included the Dickinson poems selected for *Poems, Fourth Series*, which had never appeared.

On the death of Martha Dickinson Bianchi all of her Dickinson manuscripts and other papers went to her literary collaborator Alfred Leete Hampson. Hampson sold them to a private collector, who gave them to Harvard University. Harvard's press then issued its edition of the complete poems of Emily Dickinson in three large volumes.

All of this confused and competitive issuance of additional volumes of the poetry of Emily Dickinson was furor after the fact. The basic fact had been stated when the three small volumes of her poetry and the two volumes of her letters appeared in the 1890's and her hoped-for fame was established. Emily Dickinson owes the world's knowledge and approval of her work to three women.

Helen Hunt Jackson perceived the quality of her poetry and virtually forced publication of "Success," bringing its author to the attention of the editor who finally published her work. By sheer importunity Lavinia Norcross Dickinson got her sister's major poems published. Mabel Loomis Todd selected and edited the poems with accuracy and skill.

A fourth woman was involved. She was small like the wren. Her hair was the color of the chestnut burr, and her eyes were the color of the sherry the guest leaves in the glass.

19

Owned now by Amherst College and used as a faculty residence, Emily Dickinson's home is a National Historic Site. Tourists in shorts and sweatshirts or scantier dishabille lounge and gawk in the room at the front of the mansion's upstairs hall, which she kept inviolate. In August 1971 a commemorative eight-cent Emily Dickinson stamp was issued by the United States government. "How public like a frog!"

Emily Dickinson used the mails constantly to dispatch her letters and her poems. She strained through both to tell of herself and to reach out and bring in, almost feverishly sometimes, the love and understanding for which she hungered. Though the portrait on the stamp was painted from the daguerreotype taken when she was seventeen years old, which her family did not think looked like her, a stamp to affix to her "letter to the world" seems a fitting tribute.

She wanted to make Sue and Austin proud of her someday—a long way off. The day was more distant than she imagined, but it came. Emily Dickinson is now an honored public figure, an idea she loathed. She had a different wish. She wished to write poetry of such breathtaking intensity that it would have an actual physical effect on those who read it. That wish has long since been granted. Emily Dickinson has the kind of immortality she could understand in the lives of all who have felt the power of her verse.

Emily Dickinson did not write 1,775 good poems. No one can. The sheer bulk of her poetry is as distressing as it is impressive. How lonely she must have been! There is pathos in the fact that she saved it all. Good, bad, ridiculous or sublime, it was part of her and precious to her—a comment on both her faith in the importance of what she had written and her uncertainty about it. She did not discriminate. She lacked the critical intelligence, which is not antagonistic to the creative. Like artists in other media, major poets usually have and use both.

Emily Elizabeth Dickinson never quite gave up playing at paste. She did not always know which were pearls and which were not. Some of her poems collapse after a firm line or two. Others never get started. Some of her talk of robins, bluejays, and sunsets is merely pretty. Her many moralizing poems are no better and no worse than those of many other poets. There are poems in the volumes of her verse published in the twentieth century that might better have been omitted. Like most good poets, even great ones, Emily Dickinson is better in selection than in wholesale collection.

She was not a poet of sweeping ideas. There are no grand conceptions or majestic pronouncements in her verse. Her poetry is personal and intimate. She wrote of her own innermost feelings, which she ground into excruciating fineness. Even when she wrote on large subjects —life, death, love, eternity—she wrote of them as a sensitive woman of limited experience but penetrating insight, telling what, alone, she thought and felt about them. She wrote of what many other individuals feel when they are most alone and made them feel it more deeply and with greater understanding. Because she was a poet, she touched the ordinary with magic. She makes the reader thrill to her sadness or gladness. Sharing emotions lighted by her words, those who hear or see them are for a few moments poets themselves. The note of surprise that Mabel Loomis Todd heard in Emily Dickinson's voice is in her verse too, giving it its quality of lasting freshness.

Emily Dickinson is at her best when she talks of elemental things with pungent brevity. The telling Dickinson poems are those in which she makes a flat statement in hard words or asks a pointed question with raised eyebrows. The concise comment is her forte. When in these ways she was at her best, she wrote poems that are unforgettable.

She wrote some of the most moving love poetry ever written in English, honest poems without a false note in them. She made a playfellow of God. They understood each other. She made a companion of death, but they did not understand each other at all. She lived with bobolinks, robins, and hummingbirds, with grass and hay, with day lilies and hyacinths, with college professors, politicians, and hired men, with Byron, the Brownings, George Eliot, and Shakespeare—and she defined life in just one two-syllable word.

> Surgeons must be very careful
> When they take the knife!
> Underneath their fine incisions
> Stirs the culprit—Life!

Emily Dickinson could be the sentimental spinster puttering in her garden. She could be the indulgent aunt talking baby talk to Gib, or the proper Amherst lady using gifts of flowers and confections as visiting cards for visits she did not make. Then she could turn and discover her own law of balance and compensation.

> For each ecstatic instant
> We must an anguish pay
> In keen and quivering ratio
> To the ecstasy.
>
> For each beloved hour
> Sharp pittances of years,
> Bitter contested farthings
> And coffers heaped with tears.

Emily Dickinson did not learn that from her robins, her pastry board, or bearded Amherst professors of either mental or moral philosophy. Or this:

> Pain has an element of blank;
> It cannot recollect
> When it began, or if there were
> A day when it was not.

She knew disappointment, and she could say it in her terse lines, lighten it with a homely image, and make it more deeply felt for her humor. God is a tradesman this time.

> I asked no other thing.
> No other was denied.
> I offered Being for it,
> The mighty merchant smiled.
>
> Brazil? He twirled a button.
> Without a glance my way;
> "But, madam, is there nothing else
> That we can show today?"

There was not. Emily Dickinson did not accept substitutes, and she made no concessions. She wrote her finest poetry out of scrutinizing her thoughts and sensations until, stared out of countenance, they became malleable material which she could crystallize into meaning for herself and everyone else. That is what poets do. If they have the practiced skill in their craft—and Emily Dickinson had her own—they rise through introspection to objectivity. That is, they find what seems to them the truth in their own feelings; then, in memorable form, make it truth that others can share.

Sometimes she looked around her. She sounds like Henry Thoreau here.

> The show is not the show,
> But they that go.
> Menagerie to me
> My neighbor be.
> Fair play—
> Both went to see.

When she saw what she did not like, Emily Dickinson could be annihilating.

> A face devoid of love or grace,
> A hateful, hard, successful face,
> A face with which a stone
> Would feel as thoroughly at ease
> As were they old acquaintances,—
> First time together thrown.

Emily Dickinson spent most of a hard-lived lifetime seeking her own identity. She found it. The reality of Emily Dickinson does not lie in what anyone has said or written or may say or write about her but in her verse. There she found herself, and there she is.

She kept seeking the understanding and approbation of others: Newton, Bowles, Holland, Higginson. When she got it, or as much as they could give, she usually found that she did not need it. She kept looking for what might alleviate her loneliness, then found she was lonelier when it came. Behind her pitter-patter fluttering hesitancy was a damning sureness. She was as sure that she was right in the way she lived and in her practice of poetry as her father was that he was right in all he did.

Emily Dickinson never had to face the world. She never had to earn a living. Supported and protected first by her father and then by her brother, she was free of the worries and encumbrances that hinder most people from trying to be what they wish to be or doing what they hope to do. Emily Dickinson was never forced by people or circumstance to do anything she did not wish. If she had had to compete in the outside world and learn its ways, she might well have obtained substantial recognition and reward while she lived. Then again, she might not have been able to write at all. She did not have the resilience of Helen Hunt Jackson or Mabel Loomis Todd. Perhaps, unconsciously, she knew from the beginning that she was better equipped to be a spectator than a combatant.

Except in her imagination Emily Dickinson was no wild-winging bird. She needed the brick walls of the Dickinson mansion, the high hedges, the restricted world. Mount Holyoke in her youth and Boston in her middle years had the same effect. They made her want to go home and stay there. It is no accident that she used the word "safety" to describe the door to her father's room. If had taken six generations of Amherst Dickinsons to produce her, at which point the primitive energy seems to have been exhausted. It reached both flower and full depletion in her refined intelligence. Strong in spirit as she was, Emily Dickinson had some "dimity convictions" of her own.

All she really had to do was to fit herself into life or, more accurately, for she was stubborn and determined, fit life to her. People around her had to live life on her terms. Some must have fled her, as she fled others, and escaped with relief from her intensity. If there was a great deal of worldly innocence and ignorance about Emily Dickinson, there was also an almost preternatural sharpness. She could have been a witch, only most witches do not write poetry as well.

Emily Dickinson's insistence on seclusion was a protective device. Her acute nervous sensibility demanded defense. Her reclusiveness was also instinctive and purposeful. She hoarded herself for her poetry. A thought, a feeling, or the intimation of one, a revelation, or a teasing glint of insight might be lost and wasted in conversation or mere propinquity to others. Hers was the eye turned inward and the mind that marveled at what it saw.

Was she sad? There was the material for a poem. Was she ridiculously, unexplainably happy? There was the stuff for another. Was she dull and despondent? Another poem. She watched her moods and drained them. She refined the ore, re-refined the slag, distilled the residue. Sometimes it hurt, but in this way she achieved the glory of nearly perfect expression of what she had to say.

Not for nothing had she lived with Noah Webster's lexicon during the years after Benjamin Newton's death. She found the words, she said, to every thought she ever had but one. She liked words, big words, huge words, words you can fall into—eternity, immortality, love, life, death, redemption—she used them to attain compression in severe epigrammatic lines that clamp down on the extravagance of her impetuosity. That is one of the things that gives her poetry its power.

Dimity conviction? About some things in some ways, but Emily Dickinson's love poetry is charged with frightening force. Anger bites through the cold irony in other poems. The humor rooted in her basic sanity was inextinguishable. She was concerned not with joy but with maddest joy. She was an epicure of pain and a connoisseur of agony. She disdained sobriety for emotional drunkenness. Emily Dickinson was rather a large tippler when she leaned against the sun. If her love, her anger, her laughter, or her grief had ever broken loose, they would have wiped out Amherst. The restraint she put on expression of them all enabled her to write with tense compression and to reach a blazing clarity—though even that she shot through with amethyst, topaz, and emerald.

She gave frank expression to sexual passion when it was unusual for a woman to do so, but she could hide behind the gnomic and cryptic style she adopted. Sometimes she was deliberately obscure. She did not always wish to be too clear. Someone might find her out. Dickinson discretion and Yankee parsimony sometimes battled with her generosity. She liked to mystify. It was fun. If some people did not understand, so much the better. Sometimes the obscurity sprang from impatience or contempt.

Emily Dickinson did not suffer fools or fakes gladly. She did not suffer them at all. There had to be something in a man or woman that she recognized.

Experiment to me
Is everyone I meet,
If it contain a kernel?
The figure of a nut
Presents upon a tree,
Equally plausibility;
But meat within is requisite
To squirrels and to me.

Emily Dickinson could pass her own test.

Selected Bibliography

Allen, Mary Adele. *Around a Village Green; Sketches of Life in Amherst*. Northampton, Mass.: The Kraushar Press, 1939.

An Historical Review, One Hundred and Fiftieth Anniversary of the First Church of Christ in Amherst, Massachusetts. Amherst: Press of the Amherst Record, 1890.

Anderson, Charles E. *Emily Dickinson's Poetry; Stairway of Surprise*. New York: Holt, Rinehart and Winston, 1960.

Bianchi, Martha Dickinson. *The Life and Letters of Emily Dickinson*. Boston: Houghton Mifflin Co., 1924.

Bingham, Millicent Todd. *Ancestors' Brocades, The Literary Debut of Emily Dickinson*. New York: Harper & Bros., 1945.

———— *Emily Dickinson, A Revelation*. New York: Harper & Bros., 1954.

———— *Emily Dickinson's Home, Letters of Edward Dickinson and His Family with Documentation and Coment*. New York: Harper & Bros., 1955.

Capps, Jack L. *Emily Dickinson's Reading, 1836–1886*. Cambridge: Harvard University Press, 1966.

Dickinson, Emily. *Letters of Emily Dickinson*, Mabel Loomis Todd, ed. 2 vols. Boston: Roberts Brothers, 1894. Same, new and enlarged edition. New York: Harper & Bros., 1931.

———— *Poems by Emily Dickinson,* Mabel Loomis Todd and T. W. Higginson, eds. Boston: Roberts Brothers, 1890.

———— *Poems by Emily Dickinson, Second Series,* Higginson and Todd, eds. Boston: Roberts Brothers, 1891.

———— *Poems by Emily Dickinson, Third Series,* Todd, ed. Boston: Roberts Brothers, 1896.

———— *The Poems of Emily Dickinson,* including variant readings critically compared with all known manuscripts, ed. Thomas H. Johnson. 3 vols. Cambridge: The Belknap Press of Harvard University Press, 1951, 1955.

———— *Selected Poems and Letters of Emily Dickinson,* Robert N. Linscott, ed. Garden City, N.Y.: Doubleday & Co., 1959.

Higgins, David. *Portrait of Emily Dickinson: the Poet and Her Prose.* New Brunswick, N.J.: Rutgers University Press, 1967.

Hitchcock, Frederick H. *The Handbook of Amherst, Massachusetts.* Amherst: F. H. Hitchcock, 1891.

Jenkins, MacGregor. *Emily Dickinson, Friend and Neighbor.* Boston: Little, Brown and Co., 1930.

Johnson, Thomas H. *Emily Dickinson, An Interpretive Biography.* Cambridge: The Belknap Press of Harvard University Press, 1963.

Leyda, Jay. *The Years and Hours of Emily Dickinson.* 2 vols. New Haven: Yale University Press, 1960.

Meigs, Cornelia L. *Invincible Louisa.* Alcott Centennial Edition. Boston: Little, Brown and Co., 1968.

Merriam, George S. *The Life and Times of Samuel Bowles.* 2 vols. New York: The Century Co., 1885.

Pollitt, Josephine. *Emily Dickinson, the Human Back-*

ground of Her Poetry. New York: Harper & Bros., 1930.

Taggard, Genevieve. *The Life and Mind of Emily Dickinson*. New York: Alfred A. Knopf, 1930.

Tuckerman, Frederick. *Amherst Academy; a New England School of the Past*. Amherst: Printed for the Trustees, 1929.

Ward, Theodora. *The Capsule of the Mind, Chapters in the Life of Emily Dickinson*. Cambridge: The Belknap Press of Harvard University Press, 1961.

Whicher, George Frisbie. *This Was a Poet, a Critical Biography of Emily Dickinson*. New York: Charles Scribner's Sons, 1938.

Index

A

B

C

D

W

Y